Eyes Fixed on Jesus

EYES FIXED ON JESUS

A JOURNEY INTO THE GOSPELS

VOLUME 1

MEG HUNTER-KILMER

Our Sunday Visitor
Huntington, Indiana

Nihil Obstat
Msgr. Michael Heintz, Ph.D.
Censor Librorum

Imprimatur
✠ Kevin C. Rhoades
Bishop of Fort Wayne-South Bend
January 23, 2025

The *Nihil Obstat* and *Imprimatur* are official declarations that a book is free from doctrinal or moral error. It is not implied that those who have granted the *Nihil Obstat* and *Imprimatur* agree with the contents, opinions, or statements expressed.

30 29 28 27 26 25 1 2 3 4 5 6 7 8 9

Our Sunday Visitor Publishing Division
Our Sunday Visitor, Inc.
200 Noll Plaza
Huntington, IN 46750
www.osv.com
1-800-348-2440

ISBN: 978-1-63966-302-6 (Inventory No. T2956)
1. RELIGION—Biblical Commentary—General.
2. RELIGION—Biblical Meditations—General.
3. RELIGION—Christianity—Catholic.

eISBN: 978-1-63966-303-3
LCCN: 2025936996

Cover design: Tyler Ottinger
Interior design: Amanda Falk
Cover art: J. Kirk Richards

PRINTED IN THE UNITED STATES OF AMERICA

For Rachael, whose life and death
fixed so many eyes on Jesus.

Contents

Bible Abbreviations

Old Testament

Gn	Genesis	Prv	Proverbs
Ex	Exodus	Eccl	Ecclesiastes
Lv	Leviticus	Song	Song of Songs
Nm	Numbers	Wis	Wisdom
Dt	Deuteronomy	Sir	Sirach
Jos	Joshua	Is	Isaiah
Jgs	Judges	Jer	Jeremiah
Ru	Ruth	Lam	Lamentations
1 Sm	1 Samuel	Bar	Baruch
2 Sm	2 Samuel	Ez	Ezekiel
1 Kgs	1 Kings	Dn	Daniel
2 Kgs	2 Kings	Hos	Hosea
1 Chr	1 Chronicles	Jl	Joel
2 Chr	2 Chronicles	Am	Amos
Ezr	Ezra	Ob	Obadiah
Neh	Nehemiah	Jon	Jonah
Tb	Tobit	Mi	Micah
Jdt	Judith	Na	Nahum
Est	Esther	Hb	Habakkuk
1 Mc	1 Maccabees	Zep	Zephaniah
2 Mc	2 Maccabees	Hg	Haggai
Jb	Job	Zec	Zechariah
Ps	Psalms	Mal	Malachi

New Testament

Mt	Matthew	1 Tm	1 Timothy
Mk	Mark	2 Tm	2 Timothy
Lk	Luke	Ti	Titus
Jn	John	Phlm	Philemon
Acts	Acts of the Apostles	Heb	Hebrews
Rom	Romans	Jas	James
1 Cor	1 Corinthians	1 Pt	1 Peter
2 Cor	2 Corinthians	2 Pt	2 Peter
Gal	Galatians	1 Jn	1 John
Eph	Ephesians	2 Jn	2 John
Phil	Philippians	3 Jn	3 John
Col	Colossians	Jude	Jude
1 Thes	1 Thessalonians	Rv	Revelation
2 Thes	2 Thessalonians		

Introduction

There's Something about Jesus

There's something in his message, something in his promise, something in his tenderness and his intensity, his demand for perfection, and his delight in even our weakest efforts. There's something that has captivated the world for millennia, prompting queens and mercenaries and geniuses and fools to leave all that the world has to offer in pursuit of an ancient rabbi executed as a traitor.

We get glimpses sometimes of this Jesus who makes weary hearts sing, who makes shattered lives whole. You may have no difficulty in seeing Jesus this way — as real, personal, powerful, and loving. But many of us struggle to think of him as the captivating, delightful, magnetic man described in the Gospels. Try as we might, we often perceive him as distant and uninterested, as stern and joyless, as angry and dangerous, as weak and tedious.

Perhaps blame can be laid at the feet of saccharine stained-glass images of Jesus blessing dull-eyed children, or pink-cheeked, weak-chinned portraits of Jesus looking insipid and unobjectionable. Perhaps instead it's the images of Jesus wielding the wrath of God or the ones where he looks supremely bored. Perhaps the trouble is just that the stories of the Gospel have become so familiar that we no longer allow them to penetrate us — or that they're so foreign that we've

stopped trying to enter into them. Likely we're uncomfortable with vulnerability and content to view Jesus as friendly, as pleasant, as wise in an unconvicting sort of way. So we close our ears to the wild love of God that the Gospels cry out on every page. We brush aside the intimacy of the Gospel and instead think and speak of Christ as a distant deity, forgetting how much it matters that he was made flesh and
Jn 1:14 dwelt among us.

Whatever the reason, many of us who attempt to follow Jesus see him as a vague, ethereal divinity, divorced from the true humanity through which he revealed himself to us, through which he gave himself to us. We tune out the Gospel stories we've heard so many times because we know them already, and we think we know the message they teach: God is friendly, and he likes us OK. So we nod and continue about our day unchanged. We may confess our belief in God the Son, but we've taken our eyes off Jesus.

I use the first person very deliberately here. I've followed Jesus since I was thirteen years old. I read the Bible through again and again, got degrees in theology, became a religion teacher and ultimately an itinerant evangelist. I was crazy wild in love with the Lord, yet I all but skimmed the Gospels each time I read them — dozens of times — because I thought I knew them, thought there was nothing much in there that I hadn't noticed before.

Then the Lord asked me for more. He invited me to let go of all that I thought I knew about the Gospels and fix my
Heb 12:2 eyes on *him*, to get to know him as a man, not just the Lord
Wis 11:26 and Lover of souls on whom I abstractly meditated every day.
I began to long to look in his eyes and see the smile lines that surround them. I wanted to examine the scars on his hands — not just the scars of the crucifixion but the marks from years as a carpenter, from a campfire spark, from a hard fall when he was a child learning to run.

I asked myself, what sort of man must Jesus have been? What sort of man could cause a brash fisherman to leave his
Lk 5:1–11 boat and try to learn humility? What sort of man would en-

tice a chief tax collector to make a fool of himself by climb-
ing a tree to get a better view? What sort of man could draw Lk 19:1–10
a sinful woman to bathe his feet with her tears? What sort Lk 7:36–50
of wandering preacher could attract a stolid Pharisee? What Jn 3:1–15
strength and gentleness and wisdom must have looked out from the age-old eyes in his weather-beaten face? What kinds of things made him laugh? What made him exchange knowing glances with his friends? Did he tease? Was he chatty?

I approached the Gospels again, this time with these questions in mind, and was shocked by what I'd missed in my twenty years of skimming. Over the next six months, in chapels and coffee shops from Oklahoma to Okinawa, I pored over commentaries and marked up an already well-loved Bible. I got a pencil with finer lead so that I could fit more notes into small margins. I discovered biblical context that made sense of Jesus' actions, cultural tidbits that shed new light on old stories, connections between miracles and parables and centuries of revelation offered us in the Old Testament. And these stories that had become old hat began to come alive, not just for me but for the thousands of people I preached to — people who, like me, had been tuning out the Gospels.

That's what I want to share with you here. I want to take you through the life of Christ, to break open the familiar and shed light on the foreign so that you can see the face of Jesus in these pages and learn to love him more in his word.

This book can be read from beginning to end, and I hope you take the time to do so. But it's also indexed so that if you have a particular question (or a talk or sermon or homily you need to give), you can use it as a reference book as well, looking up topics or specific passages or events in the life of Jesus. The Index of Featured Scripture Passages will direct you to the section where a passage is discussed at length, while the Index of Scripture References will point you to each time a passage appears in a margin note because it's referenced in the text. The book is also divided into chapters with a study guide at the end for those who may want

to use it for a Bible study — but promise me one thing: you will bring your Bible. You will open your Bible and read your Bible, both as you read this book and when you gather to study it in a group. You will not let this book be a substitute
Heb 4:12 for the living and effective word of God. I've done my best here (and noted which passages I'm referencing, including italicizing in each section heading the particular passage I most recommend reading), but there is simply nothing that compares to breaking open God's word. My hope is that this book will continually draw you deeper into the Scriptures themselves, and thus into the heart of God.

> *"Therefore, since we are surrounded by so great a cloud of witnesses, let us rid ourselves of every burden and sin that clings to us and persevere in running the race that lies before us while keeping our eyes fixed on Jesus, the leader and perfecter of faith."*
>
> — *Hebrews 12:1–2*

Chapter One

Preparations for the Incarnation

1. John's Prologue: John 1:1–18

The story of Jesus didn't begin on a midwinter's night in Bethlehem. It didn't begin nine months earlier in Nazareth or several thousand years earlier when Adam's sin occasioned God's promise that the Seed of the Woman would strike at the head of the serpent. In a sense, the story of Jesus never Gn 3:15
began.

That's why John's Gospel starts where it does, with impossibly complex concepts expressed in the shortest imaginable words. John wants his reader to know that, while his Gospel will focus on the life of Jesus of Nazareth, God the Son was no creation. "In the beginning," John tells us, the Word — the Son — existed. This language brings us back to the very first verse of the Bible, declaring that before God Gn 1:1
created the heavens and the earth, the Word already was. Before he's even told us the name of Jesus, John insists that we know: The Word existed before there was time. He was in relationship with God, so he was distinct from the Father, but he was God. He was divine. That one verse seems almost miraculous in its foresight. John answers centuries of heresies in fewer than twenty words.

John's purpose, though, isn't to dictate a creed but to introduce hope. "In the beginning," he says, because the world was starting over. The light of the human race, glimmering faintly in the heroes of Israel, had erupted into a flame that
Is 9:1 enlightens everyone, that calls men to be made new.

"And the Word became flesh," John cries in triumph, "and made his dwelling among us." Literally, he "pitched his tabernacle." *Tabernacle* is a word packed with meaning for Catholics, far more than we may know. Before it was a gold box on the altar, the tabernacle was the tent of God's dwell-
Ex 25:8–9 ing among the Israelites. Moses was told how to make this
abode for God, and the *shekinah*, the glory cloud indicating
Ex 40:34–35 God's presence, rested on it. From the days of Moses until
2 Mc 2:4–5 the time of Jeremiah (just before the Jews were deported and
sent into captivity in Babylon), God's presence remained in
1 Kgs 8:10–12 the Holy of Holies, the inner sanctum that was originally in
the tabernacle and later stood in the center of the Temple.
But since 587 BC, when the Temple was destroyed and Eze-
Ez 10:18; 11:23 kiel saw the Lord depart, the Jews had been without God's
presence. They had longed for him, hungered for him, and
now, in Jesus, God came to be with them again in the fullness of his glory. He fulfilled his promise to Moses ("I will
Ex 25:8 dwell in their midst") in a way that Moses could never have
imagined.

Having proclaimed the shocking Good News of the incarnation, John begins to gush, "And we saw his glory, the glory as of the Father's only Son." This language is reminiscent of the call of Abraham to sacrifice his son Isaac, "your only one, whom you love." Indeed, nearly every instance
Jer 6:26; Am 8:10; where the phrase "only son" appears in the Old Testament,
Zec 12:10 it's speaking of mourning the death of an only son. Even
when the phrase appears in reference to a daughter, it's the
Jgs 11:34; daughter of Jephthah, soon to be offered as a sacrifice to the
Tb 3:10 Lord, or Sarah, daughter of Raguel, as she prayed for death.
This phrase resounds with the threat of death; from the moment the Incarnation is announced, John is pointing us to the Cross.

This is the fullness John speaks of: the Incarnation, passion, death, resurrection, and ascension of the Son, grace poured out in place of grace. In some translations, this verse is rendered "grace upon grace," the grace of the New Covenant building on the beauty of the Old. Here Jesus, the new Moses, offers us more than merely law, as beautiful as God's law is. He offers us hearts transformed and lives given over to the Father.

For John, as for all of us, the Gospel is an invitation to experience the presence of God in a more radical way than did the Israelites, even at Sinai when God came in thunder and earthquakes and trumpet blasts. In the Incarnation, Ex 19:16–19
God comes into the darkness of our lives and brings light. He comes into the lies we believe and speaks truth. He comes into our condemnation and offers grace. He brings us to the Father.

2. The Genealogy of Jesus: *Matthew 1:1–17*; Luke 3:23–38

Like John, Matthew begins his story long before the angel declared unto Mary. Matthew isn't content with giving us the story of Jesus when we might not know how it connects to the story of Israel. So he and Luke give us genealogies of Jesus, connecting the Christ to salvation history and speaking volumes about him in the process. These two genealogies differ dramatically. Scholars have proposed various theories as to why, including a compelling (and ancient) hypothesis that Joseph was adopted and therefore one genealogy, proposed by the fourth-century historian Eusebius of Caesarea, traces Joseph's lineage through his biological father while the other considers his legal ancestry instead. But most readers today don't pay enough attention to the lists of "begats" to notice their differences; we struggle with biblical genealogies because we can't understand how they could possibly matter. Most of us are more than happy to skip the Gospel genealogies, but a moment's explanation may show that there's much to be learned about Jesus from these passages as well.

To understand just what these genealogies would have
meant to the people of Jesus' time, we have to remember that
the Jews had been waiting for their Messiah for centuries. In
587 BC, the people of Judah had been taken captive to Bab-
2 Chr 36:15–21 ylon, Jerusalem razed, and the Temple destroyed. Though
Ezr 1:1–3 some Jews returned home half a century later, it was never
the same. The new Temple was a shadow of the former, and
the people of Judah were oppressed by one world power after
another. Forty-two thousand of God's people had returned
Ezr 2:64 to their land, but the exile wasn't truly over and wouldn't be
until the Messiah liberated them and they lived in freedom,
as in the days of the great King David.

In the second century BC, the Maccabee family rebelled
against the oppressive rule of the Greeks and led the Jewish
2 Mc 2:19–22 people to freedom. Although they ruled well, they weren't of
the line of David, so the peace of their reign wasn't complete
or lasting. Later, Herod the Great put himself forward as the
Messiah, going so far as to rebuild the Temple as he sought to
secure his place. Yet Herod wasn't even an Israelite by birth,
let alone a descendant of David, and his rule did nothing to
throw off the yoke of Rome. By the time of Jesus, the people
were sick of false messiahs who promised great things but
ultimately failed to deliver. They wanted God's Anointed,
the Son of David, who would not only defeat the enemies of
Israel and restore the Temple but also establish a lasting reign
of peace. To be the true Messiah, he had to be of David's line,
unlike Herod the Pretender. Given all that, the genealogy of
any alleged Messiah would have been riveting to those who
had awaited him for centuries.

Matthew's genealogy, like his Gospel, is rooted in his
Jewish heritage. He begins with a summary: Jesus is the Son
of David, the son of Abraham. In Abraham, God had prom-
Gn 12:3 ised to bless the entire world; in Jesus, he would do just that.
Matthew traces Jesus' descent not from Adam, as Luke does,
but from Abraham, reaffirming the Messiah's identity as an
Israelite. But while Matthew traces Jesus' genealogy only to
Abraham, he begins it with "The book of the genealogy of,"

which we see in only one other place in Scripture: Genesis 5:1, the list of the descendants of Adam. In this way, Matthew links the new Adam to the old even without mentioning him. Unlike nearly every genealogy of the time, however, Matthew includes a handful of women. These women are
Bathsheba, a survivor of sexual assault; Ruth, a faithful pa- 2 Sm 11;
gan; Rahab, a prostitute; and Tamar, whose shocking story Ruth; Jos 2
can't be summarized in a word or two. Gn 38

The act of including pagan women foreshadows the universality of Jesus' mission, a call to Gentiles that would
be a stumbling block to the Jews of his day. Matthew also 1 Cor 1:23
preempts the protestations of those who might suggest that the circumstances of Jesus' birth weren't fitting for a king; if these women were honored in the lineage of kings, who could object to Mary's virginal conception?

But it's not just the women in this family tree who might leave something to be desired. Once the list moves past Solomon, it's a series of bad kings followed by a series of nobodies. And yet, in the midst of adultery and murder and idolatry and divided kingdoms and exile and drudgery, God was still working. In Zadok and Achim and Eliud, whose names we would never otherwise know, God was working. When the world was at its darkest and Israel's rulers at their cruelest, God was working.

This is more than just a list of names, however infamous or illustrious. Matthew has framed his genealogy in a way that cries out Jesus' identity as the rightful Davidic king. He begins by calling Jesus the son (or heir) of David. He then groups his genealogy into three sections, each fourteen generations long. To us, this means very little, but to Israel, fourteen was the numerical value of the name David. Thus, Jesus is the thrice Davidic king, the heir to the kingdom, the
promised Son of God whose throne will be firm forever. 2 Sm 7:13–14

While Matthew's genealogy is focused on Jesus as the promised Messiah of Israel (repeating the name of David and tracing Jesus' lineage back to Abraham), Luke presents Jesus as the savior of the whole world. Again we see Jesus' de-

scent from David, this time through Nathan rather than the
golden child Solomon (one of Luke's many ironic reversals to
show how God exalts the lowly). But Luke goes back beyond
Abraham, telling us that Jesus was "the son of Adam, the son
of God." Here in Jesus, humanity has a fresh start. As the son
of Adam, he is brother to all mankind and son to Eve, the
Gn 3:15 Son God had promised to send to destroy the serpent.

Before Adam, we would expect to see nobody since
Adam was created, not begotten. Instead, we're reminded
that Adam was the son of God. Genesis tells us that Adam
Gn 5:3 begot Seth "in his likeness, after his image." This language
clearly echoes Genesis 1, in which we're told that Adam and
Gn 1:27 Eve were created in the image and likeness of God, making
them, like Jesus, children of God (though in a far lesser way).
Jesus, then, is a new Adam and begins a new creation that
will come to fruition through the Cross, the tree of life that
Gn 3:1–7 destroys the fruit of the tree of which the first Adam ate.

Clearly, these genealogies are more than just housekeeping. They speak not just about Jesus' origins but about his mission. He has come from fallen stock to redeem and rule over Israel and all mankind, the rightful Davidic king who will bring about a new creation. With that prologue out of the way, with the stage set and our expectations raised, we can begin our story.

3. The Annunciation to Zechariah: Luke 1:5–25

Luke starts his Gospel in the heart of the Jewish world: the Temple. A righteous priest named Zechariah was serving at the Temple, while his wife, Elizabeth, waited for him at home. Though they had longed for a child for many years, the couple was barren. And while there may have been much joy in their lives, the lack of a child cast a shadow over all of it.

Still, they went on, just as we go on. As our prayers go unanswered year after year, we go about our business and try to do more than just wait. So when it was Zechariah's turn to serve at the Temple, he went. He was chosen by lot to offer incense in the sanctuary and did as was expected. Then, "when the whole assembly of the people was praying," everything changed. Held up by his community, surrounded by their prayers, Zechariah finally got an answer to his long-unanswered prayer.

There before him stood the Archangel Gabriel, just as centuries earlier he had stood before Daniel at the evening sacrifice and prophesied that a "holy of holies" or a "most holy" would come, be anointed Messiah, and be cut down. In the time of Daniel, five centuries before Zechariah's encounter, the people of God had prayed for redemption, prayed to be freed from their captivity, and Gabriel had promised that in seventy weeks of years, the deliverer would come. We'll go into this more later (in section 19, "Preaching in Galilee"), but it's worth mentioning Gabriel's prophecy in the Book of Daniel now: the Messiah would be killed 490 years after the restoration of Jerusalem following the Babylonian Captivity. The order to rebuild Jerusalem was given in the seventh year of King Artaxerxes of Persia, about 457 BC; 490 years later was AD 33. That Gabriel, who had foretold the coming of the Messiah, is also the one announcing the conception of both John the Baptist and Jesus the Christ is no coincidence.

Dn 9:21–27

Dn 9:24

Ezr 7:8

This promised Messiah had been revealed to Daniel (the archangel said) because he was beloved. Now, centuries later, Gabriel appeared again before the beloved of God to offer an answer to prayer — not merely to Zechariah's prayer but to the prayer of all God's people, a prayer for the deliverance that would be foretold by John the forerunner and won by his divine cousin. And so, after decades of hearing nothing but silence from God, Zechariah got an answer. Gabriel promised a son, a Nazirite like Sampson — a man who had made a special vow of consecration to the Lord. This son would prepare the way of the Lord, coming in the spirit of Elijah, as the prophet Malachi had foretold.

Jgs 13:3–5

Mal 3:23–34; Sir 48:10

And Zechariah doubted. This priest looked upon the terrifying face of an archangel promising him his heart's desire and doubted.

It strikes us as ridiculous. When presented with such
proof, how can you doubt? Surely after years of begging
the Lord for a child, his response should have been joy, not
skepticism. But Zechariah, like so many of us, seems to
have stopped praying in hope. He kept asking, of course —
it wouldn't do to stop asking. But he had long ago become
convinced that no matter what he did, nothing would ever
change. Elizabeth was past childbearing age, and while God
Gn 21:1–2 had given children to the elderly before, it was unreasonable
to hope that he would do it again. So gradually Zechariah's
earnest prayer had become a grudging prayer rooted in bitterness, such bitterness that when presented with a miracle,
his response was, *Prove it.*

Zechariah isn't the only man of God to have responded
that way. Abraham said much the same thing when God
promised to give him the land of Canaan. "How will I know
Gn 15:8 that I will possess it?" he responded to the vision, but — unlike Zechariah — received no curse. Instead, God cemented
his covenant with Abraham. A covenant was typically made
by sacrificing animals and then walking between their bi-
furcated remains to indicate that the one who breaks the
Jer 34:18 covenant deserves just such a fate as these animals. But God
didn't ask Abraham to walk between the split carcasses; instead, he sent a burning brazier between them, a cloud of in-
Gn 15:9–10, 17 cense that represented God himself. Rather than demanding
an oath from Abraham, God symbolically promised that if
Abraham broke this covenant, God himself would bear the
consequences.

Abraham asked for proof and received a covenant; Zechariah asked for proof and received correction. How can we
explain these opposite heavenly responses to the same question? By considering what might justly be expected of each
man. Abraham — the first of the patriarchs — was also the
first of God's people to experience a revelation of God. He
likely knew the story of Noah, but he had no real idea who
God was, or even what a god was. When God made him a
promise, he had no way of knowing if that promise would be

kept; he had every right to ask for proof. Zechariah, on the other hand, had spent his life studying the workings of God in the history of his people. He knew that God had wrought miraculous conceptions, that God had parted the Red Sea, that he had delivered his people again and again. Zechariah knew who God was. Like us, he knew that God had proven himself faithful again and again. And still he doubted.

Gn 21:1–2; Jgs 13:2–3; 1 Sm 1:1–20 Ex 14:21–22

So Zechariah's doubt was met not with proof but with punishment: He would be unable to speak "until the day these things take place." As we'll see in section 7 ("The Birth of John"), this punishment was given for his good, as God's discipline always is. In the moment, though, being unable to speak couldn't have seemed like anything but a curse. When Zechariah finally emerged from the sanctuary, to an assembly that may have been wondering if he had been struck dead within, he could only gesture to them. At this, they must have realized that something supernatural had happened. Zechariah, too, was a believer by this point (convinced by his sudden muteness if not by the sight of an archangel), but he didn't rush home to his wife to do his part in bringing about the miraculous birth that had been foretold. First, he fulfilled his duty. There's something striking about the faithfulness of a man who has witnessed an angel, been rebuked by the hand of God, and been promised an impossible answer to prayer, but finishes his job just the same.

Heb 12:11

Finally, Zechariah was released and returned home to his wife. We aren't told whether Elizabeth believed or whether he even told her, mute as he was — just that she conceived. At long last. And as her body began to show signs that she was finally a mother, she must have been transfigured by joy.

For Elizabeth, this miracle was more than just a child. Alongside Sarah the matriarch, she had struggled through decades of pain and longing, but also decades of shame. To many in the ancient world, women were only as valuable as the children they could produce, and being barren was often viewed as the result of a woman's sin. "The Lord has seen fit to take away my disgrace," Elizabeth cried out with Rachel,

Gn 16—21

Gn 30:23 the wife of Jacob and mother of Joseph. She had struggled
with infertility as so many do, wrestling with grief and guilt and shame. Perhaps over the years she had accepted this disgrace as something she deserved.

But in all those years of sorrow and shame, God had been working. He had been planning. He had been waiting to answer Elizabeth's earnest prayer, waiting until the
exact moment when the child he gave her could become the
Mt 11:11 greatest prophet ever born. What had seemed an unanswered
prayer was really an answer beautiful beyond imagining, as Elizabeth would begin to understand in the coming months. Even when God had appeared to be silent and distant, he had been at work in her life, preparing a joy to redeem all her suffering. Not even Zechariah's obstinate doubt could get in the way of the beautiful plan God had for their joy.

Chapter Two

The Word Made Flesh in Mary's Womb

4. The Annunciation: Luke 1:26–38

Finally, we've come to Jesus, to the little house in the nowhere village in backwater Galilee where a young woman was going about her business like any ordinary day. Simply from this setting we see that God was flipping the world on its head. John's birth had been announced to a priest in the Temple in Jerusalem, the center of the world. But John was only the forerunner. The Messiah — whose sandal strap John wasn't worthy to untie — was announced to a peasant girl in an unknown town in an unimportant region. Luke tells us that God's ways are not our ways by pointing out these ironic reversals, and we would do well not to judge him by our standards. Jn 1:27 Is 55:8

Here, in the most unexpected of places, everything changed. We had wandered lost for thousands of years and finally, *finally*, God was coming to save us, to empty himself and take the form of a slave. He did it by asking a girl for permission to work in her life. "Hail," Gabriel said, though the word might be better translated "rejoice." Rejoice! What better word to announce the coming of the Desired of all nations, the end of darkness and the dawn of everlasting joy? Phil 2:7 Hg 2:7; Ps 65:6

Then Gabriel addressed the Blessed Mother, not by her given name, but with a title — or, perhaps, by the name God calls her: *you who have been made grace.* This was not the imposing Gabriel of a few verses past, standing imperiously before a terrified Zechariah. Here, God's archangel bowed before the woman who would become God's mother, saying, "The Lord is with you." This greeting sounds like a platitude to our ears, an echo of the priest's greeting at Mass. We almost expect Mary to respond, "And with your spirit."

Instead, she was troubled. It stands to reason that Mary knew the Scriptures better than anyone. Her mind untainted by sin was clear and focused in a way the greatest minds of sinful man have never been. She had studied the Scriptures (even if only by listening well), and she knew that when God promised to be with someone in this way, it usually meant that difficult times were coming. "I will be with you," the Lord had said to Jacob before sending
Gn 31:3 him back to the brother he had supplanted. "I will be with
Ex 3:12 you," to Moses when calling him to stand against Pharaoh.
"I will be with you," to Joshua as he led the grumbling Is-
Dt 31:23; Jos 1:5 raelites to take possession of the Promised Land. To Gide-
Jgs 6:12, 16 on going into battle, to Jeroboam splitting the kingdom,
1 Kgs 11:38 again and again this promise of God reads almost like a
threat. *I will be with you, because otherwise there's no way you would survive what is to come.* Only now does Gabriel urge Mary to have no fear, now that his message has begun to make her wonder what exactly might be in store.

Mary couldn't have been terribly reassured when the angel told her the purpose of his mission: to make her the mother of the Son of the Most High, the Davidic king who would reign not just over Judah but over the whole house of Jacob, the entirety of fragmented Israel (and all the world, as she would soon discover). Mary was told that her son would
2 Sm 7:16 reign forever — not just his line but *him*. She learned that he
would be God's Son. But she asked no questions about any of that. Instead, she asked a question that no betrothed woman should need to ask when told of an impending pregnancy:

"How?"

Again, it looks like the same question as Zechariah's. But Mary's was different. The angel didn't punish her; he explained himself. Zechariah wanted proof, but Mary wanted instruction. Her question makes sense only if Mary and Joseph hadn't intended to have the sort of marriage that produces children. The early Church believed that their marriage had been contracted with the understanding that Mary would remain a virgin. This tradition was already well-established by the mid-second century, when the Protoevangelium of James described Mary's life as a sort of consecrated virgin, dedicated to the Lord at the age of three and living in the Temple until she reached adolescence and was betrothed to Joseph in a virginal marriage. If this was the case, Mary's question is perfectly logical. *How will I conceive? Is God dispensing me of my intended celibacy, or is something else going on?*

Gabriel explained, using the same language that described the *shekinah*, the glory cloud of God's presence that
came upon his holy dwelling in the desert. "The power of the Ex 40:34–35
Most High will overshadow you," he said, using a verb that a Jew steeped in Scripture could never hear without thinking
of the presence of God in the Ark of the Covenant within the 1 Kgs 8:10–12; Ex
Holy of Holies. The word translated here as "overshadow" is 25:21–22
found in the Gospels only here and at the Transfiguration. Mt 17:5; Mk 9:7;
In the moment of her conception, Mary would become the Lk 9:34
dwelling place of God himself, more even than the Ark of the Covenant had been. The child she would bear would
be the Son of God, a title not merely indicating God's favor Ps 2:7
upon the king (as that term was often used) but a statement of eternal truth: the Son of God, begotten of the Father. And then Gabriel offered Mary's cousin, not as proof but as companionship: Elizabeth, too, had conceived. *You will not be alone in this. Just as the Father has sent John as the forerunner, Elizabeth has gone before you in this miracle, this joy and wonder tainted by wagging tongues. The God who opens barren wombs will now open a virgin's womb, "for nothing will be*

impossible for God."

For Mary, there was no need for deliberation, no need to wonder what Joseph might say, what her parents might say, what her village might say. She had lived her life in pursuit of the Father, and when he called, she ran after him. *I'm God's servant girl,* she said. *He can do whatever he likes with me. Fiat mihi secundum verbum tuum.*

That fiat was the first of a thousand fiats that Mary would offer to the Father. In accepting his will that day in Nazareth, she was saying yes to Bethlehem, to Egypt, to Calvary. Each time, she embraced the Father's will once again. A life of discipleship isn't a matter of one moment's conversion, but a thousand conversions, a thousand fiats offered to the Lord.

And the Word was made flesh. And we were no longer alone, no longer lost and stumbling, no longer desperate for hope in a hopeless world. God was coming for his children,
Lk 19:10 coming to seek and save the lost.

5. Joseph's Reaction: Matthew 1:18–24

One wonders what Mary did after the angel left her. Did she sit for hours in ecstatic prayer? Run off to pore over the Scriptures to discover what had been said about the tiny Messiah growing within her? Search eagerly — or nervously — for her parents to tell them the news? Did she ask Joachim to speak to Joseph, or did she tell him herself? Did she expect anyone to believe her? Did she anticipate their doubt? On all of this, Scripture is silent.

The next thing we hear is Joseph's reaction. Mary was "found with child" when she was betrothed to him, something much stronger than an engagement today. Legally, she was his wife, though they weren't yet living together and the marriage hadn't been consummated.

So when he discovered that this beautiful, holy, virginal girl was pregnant, a girl who had asked him to promise a celibate marriage, Joseph must have been heartbroken. There are two major views on Joseph's reaction in the tradition of the Church. One is that Joseph believed Mary's story from the start but didn't feel worthy to be the foster father of the Messiah. According to this understanding, the angel who later appears to him calls him "Son of David" to remind him of his dignity and to strengthen him to do what he must as Jesus' father on earth. Others (including Saints Augustine, Ambrose, and John Chrysostom) assert that disbelief would have been an entirely reasonable response on Joseph's part. Though both views are worthy of meditation, the latter is particularly compelling given that Joseph seems to have felt conflicted over handing Mary over to a punishment that she (seemingly) deserved. If this was the case, Joseph's heartbreak was more than the ordinary anguish of a husband betrayed; he had thought Mary pure as no other woman had ever been pure. When she turned up pregnant and with a ridiculous story about an angel, it must have nearly destroyed him. However he may have tried to believe her, the idea of a pregnant virgin was just ridiculous in a world before Christmas carols. Her story simply couldn't be true. The heartbroken carpenter knew he couldn't live his life with such a woman. Still, he loved her. And if he exposed her infidelity to their neighbors, she would be stoned. He couldn't let that happen.

So Joseph became the bad guy. Rather than tell the world of Mary's apparent betrayal, he chose to look like a man who would divorce his pregnant wife. There is so much of Saint Joseph's character in this choice, and even some of Christ's: to save his unworthy beloved, he chose to take her shame upon himself.

Joseph can't be blamed for his disbelief, if disbelief it was — what man hearing such a story could fail to doubt it? Though he must have reproached himself for it time and again in the years that followed, what matters in Joseph's reaction wasn't his inability to accept the impossible but his willingness to accept the cross. When he thought himself betrayed, he didn't seek revenge; this righteous man sought to serve.

Resigned to his fate — and grieving the loss of the future

he'd dreamed of — Joseph fell into sleep, where he found
Gn 37:5–11 (like another Joseph long before) that his dreams spoke more
truth than his waking. An angel assured him that the unbelievable tale he'd been told was God's own truth: This child was conceived by the Holy Spirit. The angel addressed Joseph as Son of David, thus pointing out that Joseph was no mere placeholder, no convenient bachelor who could help the Blessed Mother avoid scandal. In standing as the earthly father of Jesus, Joseph made his son the heir of David.

To Joseph also came the first revelation of Jesus as Savior. Mary was told that he would be the true Son of God, the Davidic King. But Joseph was told the meaning of his name, and hence his deepest identity: "You are to name him Jesus, because he will save his people from their sins." The name
Jesus means "God saves," a translation of the name Joshua,
Jos 1:1–2 who led his people into the Promised Land. It may also be a
reference to the promise that on the day of the Lord, when
Is 25:9 God would provide a feast for all peoples, the people would
behold the God who had saved them. But the angel didn't say that *God the Father* would save his people. He said that *Jesus* would. And if the name "God saves" meant the child would save his people, then Jesus is both the Savior and God himself.

All this, we're told, was in fulfillment of Isaiah's prophecy that a virgin would conceive and bear a child called Em-
Is 7:14 manuel, God with us. It's a prophecy that seems so clearly
to promise the virgin birth — to those of us with hindsight, that is. Had we never heard of such a thing as a virgin conceiving, we, like Joseph, would have thought it absurd. Considered on its own, Isaiah's prophecy doesn't seem terribly Messianic. And while "virgin" is one way of translating it, it can also be read as saying that a "young woman" would conceive, something not at all unusual. This being the more logical understanding, it was the accepted interpretation of the passage — until the New Testament cast light on the Old, and the Old was revealed to be much more than it seemed.

For Joseph, the testimony of the angel was proof enough.

As soon as he awoke, he did as he had been told. He who had grieved over the loss of his bride now obeyed the Lord without hesitation, and through the faithfulness of this strong, meek man, this occasion of deep pain was transfigured into the joy of being the husband of the Blessed Mother and the father of God Incarnate.

6. The Visitation: Luke 1:39–56

Now reconciled to Joseph, Mary set off in haste to meet Elizabeth and accompany her on this beautiful, joyful, painful path — and to have a companion herself.

But though Mary and Elizabeth must surely have strengthened and supported each other through their unexpected pregnancies and the scandals that each must have provoked, this story is about more than just the importance of community.
Luke's tale is shot through with echoes of the Old Testament,
most especially surrounding the Ark of the Covenant, which
had been the place of God's presence among his people un- Ex 25:21–22
til the Ark was hidden before the Babylonian Captivity began
in the sixth century BC. Mary arose and went to Judah, just 2 Mc 2:4–5
as David and his companions had gone to retrieve the Ark in
order to bring it to Jerusalem; the Greek is identical to the Sep- 2 Sm 6:2
tuagint verse referring to David, and Luke uses the word *Judah*
here to match the earlier passage, rather than his usual *Judea*.
John the Baptist leaped in his mother's womb just as David
danced before the Ark. "How does this happen to me, that 2 Sm 6:14
the mother of my Lord should come to me?" Elizabeth asked, 2 Sm 6:9
echoing the words of David about the Ark. Even the word for
Elizabeth crying out in a loud voice is used in the Septuagint
only about praise of God, specifically when worshipping before 1 Chr 15:28; 16:4
the Ark.

Luke's purpose is clear: to show that Jesus is God himself, the same one whose presence was contained within the Ark, God from God, light from light, true God from true God. In Jesus, the incarnate God of Israel, we see a fulfillment of the Old Testament, not a repudiation or a replacement. And in Mary, as in the Ark, we see one whose holiness was bestowed on her by the one she bore within her.

Somehow, Elizabeth grasped some hint of all this before she had even heard Mary's story. Prompted by the Spirit, she believed, responding to the Blessed Mother as one responded to the Ark of the Covenant, the dwelling of the presence of God. Elizabeth called Mary "the mother of my Lord," a title proper to the queen mother and (as such) foreign to the Jewish people of her time, as they had been without a real king for centuries. Elizabeth's encounter with the unborn Christ child was not just a personal encounter with God but another step in the restoration of Israel, the kingdom of God.

"Blessed are you who believed!" cried the wife of the
Lk 1:18 man who had not believed. And yet we see no trace of correction for her husband here. There is only wonder at Mary's faith, a faith echoed here by one who knew what it was to have a prayer answered.

Elizabeth's proclamation doesn't just identify Mary as the Ark of the Covenant and queen mother; the verse we're most likely to gloss over proclaims Mary's identity as far more than a docile young woman. "Most blessed are you among women!" Elizabeth cried out. Many of us have prayed this line fifty-three times a day for most of our lives. But it would have been familiar to Mary, too. Twice before, this praise had rung out for a woman in the Old Testament:
Jgs 4:17–22; 5:24 for Jael, the wife of Heber, who had slaughtered Israel's en-
Jdt 13:4–10, 18 emy in his sleep, and for Judith, the widow who had done the same.

Mary may well have been sweet and simple and quiet, as she is often depicted, but she was also a warrior. She was the New Eve, bearing the One who would defeat the enemy of
Gn 3:15 God's people. By her fiat, she struck at the head of the serpent, just as Jael struck at Sisera and Judith at Holofernes. Her meek submission was an act of violent rebellion against the tyranny of sin.

This act of faith from Elizabeth stirred Mary's heart,
1 Sm 2:1–10 and she broke into a song that echoes that of Hannah, the mother of Samuel, another Israelite woman whose womb

God had opened. Mary sang her Magnificat in a spirit of absolute humility. When Elizabeth praised her for her faith, Mary praised God for blessing her in her lowliness. This is true humility: not to deny the good things God has done in and through us, but to offer praise to him for all those gifts.

After praising God for blessing her in her lowliness, Mary began to speak of the power of God to turn the world upside down, to exalt the lowly and cast down the mighty. It's a theme we'll see throughout the Gospels: the reversal of the world's values. So often people believe that those who live on the streets or single mothers or those who use wheelchairs or those who live with mental illness or addiction somehow deserve their misfortune. But Mary proclaimed the good news that God's love reaches down to sinners and outcasts — and that in his love, he rebukes the powerful.

Ps 146:8–9

In looking at the poetry here, we see balanced pairs: cast down the mighty and lifted up the lowly; filled the hungry and sent the rich away empty. The third in the series is deliberately unfinished, though: God has helped Israel, she says. But he has not destroyed the Gentiles, the logical complement. Israel wasn't being redeemed at the expense of their enemies; rather, Israel was being redeemed for the salvation of their enemies. Many Jews at the time of Jesus had no desire for God to work good for the pagan nations (many of whom were their enemies and oppressors), in spite of the Old Testament promises that the Gentiles would come to worship the God of Israel. But nowhere did Jesus bow before the demands and expectations of the people, in this or any other matter. He came not just for the sons of Abraham but for all men, as he would make clear from the moment of his birth.

Is 2:2–3; 11:10; Mi 4:1–2; Zec 2:15; 8:20–23

7. The Birth of John: Luke 1:57–80

Luke tells us that Mary remained with Elizabeth for three months and then went home. Following that tidy conclusion to Mary's visit, we see the birth of John, and our modern, Western minds assume that Mary must have left before John was born. This would put her walking out the door

2 Sm 6:11

just as Elizabeth was on the point of giving birth, since she'd come in Elizabeth's sixth month.

Ancient biographies weren't written as modern ones are written, though. The ancients saw their purpose as expressing the meaning of a life, not a play-by-play of every event, and so they grouped events by theme, not by strict chronology. Because of this, we can't always know exactly what order gospel events happened in, but we also don't need to be concerned when the order of events varies between Gospels. The question isn't "Who's right?" but "What point is the Evangelist trying to make? What is the Spirit saying here?" Here, Luke has finished with his story of Mary for the moment, so he concludes it and moves on to the next: the birth of John. Mary must have remained with Elizabeth for his birth, supporting her elderly cousin through a painful and exhausting labor.

Difficult as it must have been, John's birth was an occasion of great joy for Elizabeth and her neighbors. For Zechariah, though, there may have been some misgivings. He had been struck mute by the angel and told that his affliction
Lk 1:20 would continue "until the day these things take place." As
Elizabeth's time drew near, Zechariah was surely eager to meet his son, but also to regain his voice.

And then John was born. And Zechariah was still mute.

Had God forgotten him? Had his repentance been insufficient? Would he remain mute forever?

Zechariah's inability to speak was more than just the extreme inconvenience it would be today. There was no texting, no sign language. Paper was precious, not to be wasted on daily communication, and many were illiterate anyway. Even if someone had the patience to wait for him to write on a slate, Zechariah could say little.

And his silence changed his status. Here we have a priest, educated in the things of God, respected by his community. But when he turned up mute, people gradually started ignoring him — they even named his child without consulting him, as though he didn't exist anymore. And when they did consult him, they did it by making signs rather than speaking. Since he couldn't talk, they dismissed him as senile or possibly assumed he was deaf as well. Whatever their belief about his silence, the result was the same: Zechariah had held a prominent place in his community, and now he was an afterthought. But the angel had told him this wouldn't last forever, so Zechariah fixed his eyes on the light at the end of the tunnel. *Only nine months*, he would have thought, counting down the days to the birth of John and Zechariah's own restoration to his community.

Then, nothing. And what was he to think? Only that his voice was gone forever. After his confusion and anger and frustration when he remained mute, Zechariah must have asked himself: *Is it worth it? Is this child worth it? When I offered that prayer for so many years, was I willing to accept its answer at so great a cost?*

Ultimately, the question was this: *Do I trust God? As hard as this is, do I trust him? When he seems to have forgotten me, do I trust him?*

That was the question to which he had given a resound-
ing "No" in the Temple. But on the day of John's circumci- Lk 1:18
sion, Zechariah had another chance. When Elizabeth named the baby John and the neighbors protested, Zechariah could have written in bitterness that they should name the baby after him. If he couldn't speak, he ought at least to get something out of this. But Zechariah had spent ten months in silence, pondering all that God had done, not just for him but for his people over the centuries. And because he finally understood how faithful God is, Zechariah was faithful, too. Though he couldn't be sure that his voice would return, he knew what he had been told to do. He knew the baby was to be named John.

"John is his name," he wrote, and with that act of trust in the darkness, Zechariah's tongue was loosed, and he began to prophesy, proclaiming a hymn of victory. God has brought redemption, he cried, salvation and mercy!

Looking back, we might object, "He's done nothing of

the sort! Jesus hasn't even been born yet, let alone died or risen. You're shouting hallelujahs in Advent — try not to get ahead of yourself."

But Zechariah knew what he was doing. He knew that somehow, the conception of Mary's baby had begun a chain of events that would certainly end Israel's exile and fulfill God's promises to his people. So Zechariah praised God for what he was about to do, then turned to his infant son, proclaiming John's vocation as the forerunner of the Messiah,
Mal 3:1, 23 the messenger sent to prepare the way of the Lord. Zechariah's words demonstrate just how much God had taught him during his forced ten-month retreat, particularly when he pointed out that Jesus would save his people not from their oppressors (which was the deeply held desire of every faithful Jew) but from their sin.

"The daybreak from on high will visit us," he proclaimed, using a Messianic title found in the Septuagint translation of
Zec 3:8; 6:12; Jer the book of his predecessor, Zechariah the prophet. That this
23:5 dawn would bring light to those dwelling in darkness recalls
Jn 1:5 the imagery from the beginning of the Gospel of John. It's unlikely that Zechariah understood all that the Spirit had enabled him to proclaim, but he and his family were certainly beginning to see that Jesus would be much more than anyone had expected: liberator, savior, Messiah, dawn from on high. Jesus.

Chapter Three

The Christmas Story

8. The Birth of Jesus: Matthew 1:25; *Luke 2:1–7*

The birth of Jesus may well be the story most repeated in all of human history. We all know it, don't we? The census and Mary on the donkey and no room at the inn and the ox and ass in the cozy, warm stable, a sweet little fable all wrapped up in a candy cane-striped bow.

But the story is, of course, more complicated and terrible and beautiful than our pageants allow. Once again, we're relying entirely on Luke, who knows more about the inner workings of the Blessed Mother's life and heart than he possibly could without having spent time with her. Luke is telling Mary's story.

He's also telling the story of a conquering Messianic king turning the world on its head.

Luke begins the story of Christmas with the announcement of a census ordered by Caesar Augustus. His mention of Caesar here is more than just a detail laid down by a historian. Luke is evoking Augustus's image while setting the stage for the birth of Jesus. Augustus was the first emperor of Rome, the man who united the Romans after years of strife and established the *pax Romana*, the peace of Rome.

That alone would be enough to invite parallels to Jesus

— a ruler who unites the people and brings peace. But Rome had declared Augustus to be far more than just a peace-bringer. Augustus's predecessor and adoptive father, Julius Caesar, had been declared divine after his death, making Augustus the "son of god." More than that, Augustus was himself considered a god and the savior of men. A famous inscription at Priene in Western Turkey, written about 9 BC, says, "The birthday of the god Augustus was the beginning of the good tidings [*euangelion* or Gospel] for the world that came by reason of him." Here we have an anti-Messiah: an alleged son of god who conquers nations by the sword, bringing the dubious peace of oppression and calling himself the savior, a false god whose birth was considered Gospel, or good news. All this was evoked by the mere mention of his name.

And now this pretender, the most powerful man in the world, was calling the whole world to be enrolled. The stage is set: Under Rome, the world had been united as never before. After the true king was born, the Good News would spread through the united empire like wildfire. The same imperial structure that required this census would also make possible the offer of salvation that would go out to all the world a few decades later. Through his census, Augustus became an agent in the plan of God, orchestrating the Messi-
Mi 5:1 ah's birth in Bethlehem (as it had been prophesied) and thus
paving the way for the true peace that would come through the baby in the manger.

None of this was on the minds of Mary and Joseph. For them, it was simply a matter of getting to Bethlehem. Perhaps Joseph had been born there or still had property there. Surely King David hadn't been his last ancestor to live there, as "return to the home of your earliest royal ancestor" isn't a terribly logical direction for a census. But whatever the earthly reason, the eternal reason had been written before the
Ps 90:2 mountains were born and the earth and the world brought
forth: Bethlehem was the city of David, and from Bethlehem the Son of David must come. In Bethlehem (which means
Jn 6 "house of bread") must be born the one who would be bro-

ken to feed his people.

That night in Bethlehem, the God who had deigned
to become one of us debased himself still further. He could
have been born a king, waited on by countless slaves, suffering the indignities of human life but with some measure
of comfort and ceremony. But God chose instead to be one
with us in the poverty and weakness of our lives. He was Phil 2:7
born in a stable and laid in a feed trough, his body in the
manger foreshadowing his body given as our food. He came
in weakness, all his strength bound up in the helpless humanity of a newborn who couldn't even control his flail-
ing arms. When half-spent was the night, he fulfilled the
prophecy of the Book of Wisdom, itself a remembrance of
the Exodus: "For when peaceful stillness encompassed ev- Wis 18:14–15
erything / and the night in its swift course was half spent,
/ Your all-powerful word from heaven's royal throne / leapt
into the doomed land." The cries of that babe ought to have
cast terror into the heart of the Evil One, but as yet the powers of hell had no idea what losses they would suffer at the
hands of the infant lying in a manger.

"There was no room for them in the inn," Luke says, a
line that ought to evoke deep sorrow in our hearts. God was
made man for us, but we would not make room for him. "He
came to what was his own, but his own people did not accept Jn 1:11
him." Throughout his life, this refrain reechoed: "The Son
of Man has nowhere to rest his head." When we had forgot- Mt 8:20
ten that this world is not our home, he left the bosom of the
Father and became homeless to remind us that we are merely
pilgrims longing to find our way home. Heb 11:13

The wood of that manger points to the wood of the
cross. Mary wrapped her baby boy in swaddling clothes
and laid him in a manger, just as St. Joseph of Arimathea
would later wrap him in a linen cloth and lay him in a rock- Lk 23:53
hewn tomb. Here in the peaceful stillness of Bethlehem, we
remember Calvary, knowing that Jesus' Incarnation was always drawing him to his passion, death, and resurrection,
his life offered for us from the very beginning as he handed

himself over for our salvation.

And so the King of kings was born in squalor, the Light of the world breaking forth in darkest night. And when Love was spurned and rejected, he offered himself just the same, as much in the manger as he did on the cross, because God would stop at nothing to save his beloved — to save you.

From heaven he'd called and shouted, sending patriarchs, prophets, and psalmists, but his children — who were
looking for him in every starry sky or pagan shrine or mar-
ket or embrace — couldn't hear his love thundering through
Bar 3:34–35 creation. Since the dances of the stars weren't enough, he
sent one star. Since his words of love weren't enough, he sent
one Word. And on that barren night in Bethlehem, the long-
awaited Messiah came quietly into the world to whisper the
words of love he had been shouting since the earth was a
Gn 1:2 formless wasteland. The Dawn from on high shone on those
Lk 1:78–79 who dwelt in darkness and the shadow of death. And the
world has never been the same.

9. Angels Appear to the Shepherds: Luke 2:8–20

For a few moments, Mary and Joseph worshipped their son in the quiet of the stable. But this good news couldn't be silenced, and suddenly an angel appeared in dazzling glory to shepherds in the fields — to poor men who garnered little respect from the rest of society. When Christ the Good Shepherd was born in poverty, his birth wasn't announced to kings and priests, but to ordinary, humble men. And though they were struck with great fear, they listened to the angel's message and followed without hesitation.

The angel cried out the good news, the *euangelion* of
the coming of Christ, bringing joy not just to Jews but to
"all the people." Here Luke uses the same word that inau-
gurates Mark's Gospel, the word that is so familiar to us:
Mk 1:1 *euangelion* (*evangelium* in Latin) — Gospel. This term has
been so thoroughly baptized that it sounds to us like a word
that has no meaning outside the Christian context, but the
evangelists were borrowing a term from the rulers of their

day. When the Romans won a decisive battle, they were in the habit of sending messengers to conquered territories with an announcement (*euangelion*) proclaiming the good news that they had arrived bringing peace (or, rather, subjugating the people). When Luke and Mark use this word, it's another ironic reversal, a declaration that it's not the mighty emperor of Rome who brings peace but the infant in the manger, the wandering carpenter. But it's also another fulfillment of promises made in the Old Testament, specifically
Isaiah's prophecies of the "good news" that the Lord God Is 40:9–10
would be present among his people, ruling as king and as the Is 52:7
Good Shepherd who carries the lambs close to his heart. The Is 40:11
same root word appears in Isaiah's prophecy that the nations
would come to Zion bearing gold and frankincense, and in Is 60:6; Mt 2:11
the Messianic prophecy that Jesus himself quoted when he
stood up to preach in the synagogue at Nazareth. Even un- Is 61:1; Lk 4:18
educated shepherds knew that this "good news" proclaimed by the angels was earth-shattering, empire-toppling, world-redeeming news.

The angel must have shocked the shepherds even more when he proclaimed that the Messiah would be found not clothed in extravagant garments and resting in a palace, but wrapped in swaddling clothes and lying in a manger — a
sign to be contradicted indeed. But the Messiah had been Lk 2:34
promised, and the writings of Daniel foretold that his coming was nigh, so the shepherds who dwelt in David's city Dn 9:21–27
received the news as news of joy.

Luke's account strikes us as sweet, but it's truly subversive. He announces Jesus with the language of an imperial edict, calling him Lord and Savior (two titles that belonged to Caesar). Then he describes the angels as a "host," a term generally used for soldiers and armies. He comes in humility, this Prince of Peace, but his coming will shake the foundations of the world.

But the angels sang only of peace and of glory to God, and then disappeared, leaving the shepherds with much to consider. In haste they made their way to the stable where the baby lay. Did they worship? Did Mary hand them her baby to hold? We can't know. But when they heard the news of Jesus, they sought him and then proclaimed him.

No longer were Mary and Joseph left in silence with the
infant God — all who heard were amazed and must have
come to see this wondrous thing. These others did not behold the dazzling light or the angels singing "Gloria." No,
they saw only a young family bedded down in a stable and
heard only the testimony of a handful of shepherds. They
were amazed, indeed, but the word doesn't necessarily imply
belief or delight. The apostles would later be "amazed" when
Jn 4:27 they found Jesus speaking with a Samaritan woman, and
Mk 15:5 Pilate was "amazed" at Jesus' silence during his trial. Some
in Bethlehem that day may have ridiculed the story, others
may have been confused. Certainly, whatever reaction they
had didn't last long enough for anyone to remember it thirty
years later when the son of Joseph began doing unexplainable things. Like many of us, they had an encounter with
Jesus and a strong reaction — and then went on their way
unchanged.

And what of the shepherds, these first evangelists who
gave testimony to the Christ child and gave praise to God?
Ordinary shepherds, they had been invited to bow before
1 Sm 16:11–13 the Good Shepherd in the city of the shepherd-turned-king.
These men whom the world viewed as beneath notice were
the first called to witness to the Messiah. We would expect
them to be forever changed. They might just as easily look
at us — chosen, called, redeemed — and expect the same.

10. The Circumcision and the Presentation: Luke 2:21–38

Luke the Gentile now leads us through a series of very Jewish events: the circumcision, the redemption of the firstborn,
and the purification of the mother. The first went entirely
according to plan: As with every Hebrew boy since Abra-
Gn 17:9–14 ham, the mark of the covenant was cut into the flesh of Jesus.
Here, God's blood was first shed in faithfulness to the will of

the Father, as those first few drops of blood became a promise of his blood poured out for us on the cross.

Then the Holy Family seems to have passed a few mercifully quiet weeks — though with the town all abuzz about the shepherds' testimony, it couldn't have been terribly private. Still, they seem not to have traveled again until Jesus was forty days old, when the family journeyed six miles to the Temple in Jerusalem.

Luke does an interesting thing here: He says Jesus was
being presented to the Lord "just as it is written in the law
of the Lord, 'Every male that opens the womb shall be consecrated to the Lord.'" During the Exodus, God declared all Ex 13:2, 12
firstborn sons to be sacred, consecrated to him because he
had rescued them from the angel of death during the tenth Ex 13:15
plague in Egypt. But after the incident of the golden calf in
the desert, when the Levites rose up against their brethren Ex 32:25–29
to defend God's honor, an exchange was made: All Levites
would be sacred to God, while all other firstborn sons would Nm 3:12–13
be ransomed by an offering of five silver coins. Nm 18:16

For most Israelites it seemed a purely symbolic exchange; in the case of Jesus, his being consecrated to the
Father was far more than a symbol. And indeed, there is
no evidence that he was ransomed. The exchange was to be
made when a baby boy was a month old, but Luke doesn't Nm 18:16
tell of a trip until twelve days later. Even then, there were
no coins, no "buying back" of the firstborn. Instead, baby
Jesus was offered to the Lord just as young Samuel had 1 Sm 1:24–28
been, consecrated to the Father's service. Mary and Joseph
knew that their firstborn son was the only begotten Son of
God. He was already dedicated to the Lord, the great high Gn 14:18–20; Ps
priest of the order of Melchizedek instead of Levi; there 110:4;
was no need to ransom him. And so Mary, who had echoed Heb 5:5–10
Hannah's song of praise, now stood, just as Hannah had, Lk 1:46–55;
to offer her young son to the Lord. 1 Sm 2:1–10

This sacrifice of her son wasn't the only oblation Mary had brought that day. The young family had come to the Temple to offer a sacrifice for the purification of the Blessed

Lv 12:2–8 Mother, as required by the Mosaic law. Here, as in all things,
the Holy Family was absolutely obedient to the law — Luke
makes this abundantly clear, repeating five times in this
Lk 2:22, 23, 24, chapter that the Holy Family acted in accordance with the
27, 39 law of Moses. Jesus would have belonged to the Father even
without circumcision, but he was circumcised just the same.
Joseph didn't need to visit the Temple each Passover when he
Mt 12:6 had "something greater than the temple" living in his home,
but he did. It wasn't a matter of keeping up appearances, but
a desire to be faithful to the covenant of the Lord, to enter
fully into all that it meant to be God's people.

It was this faithfulness that first brought the Lord to the
Temple, quietly fulfilling the prophecy of Malachi, "And the
Mal 3:1; Hg 2:7 LORD whom you seek will come suddenly to his temple."
Nearly six centuries earlier, Ezekiel had seen the glory of the
Ez 10:18; 11:23 Lord departing from the Temple, leaving God's house deso-
Jer 52:12–14 late even before it was destroyed by the Babylonians. For six
centuries, the Jewish people had longed for the Lord to re-
turn to their midst. When he finally did, it wasn't surround-
ed by cherubim and trumpet blasts with throngs of adoring
worshippers, but carried by a peasant couple and greeted by
nobody but an old man and a widow. God's ways are not our
Is 55:8 ways, nor can we always see when he is moving.

But in every age, there are people whose vision is clearer than most, people whose eyes and hearts are fixed on God. Simeon was just such a man, "righteous and devout, awaiting the consolation of Israel, and the holy Spirit was upon him." Here was a man whose heart was hungry for the coming of the Lord, who woke each day wondering if this would be the day that he would see the Messiah.

In the Eastern Church, there is a tradition that Simeon was more than just a pious old man. He was, they say, one of the scholars who had been invited to translate the Old Testament into Greek in the third century BC — the translation now known as the Septuagint (abbreviated LXX). Tradition has it that all seventy scholars miraculously came back with the exact same translation of the entire Old Testament ex-

cept for one man who couldn't fathom the idea that a virgin
will be with child. He insisted on using another word that Is 7:14
clearly just meant young woman, at which an angel appeared to him and told him that he wouldn't see death until he saw this prophecy fulfilled.

According to this legend, Simeon would have been some 300 years old at the time of the Presentation. He would have seen his friends, his wife, his children, and his great-great-great-grandchildren die. He would have been old and tired and incredibly lonely. He would have had nothing else to live for but this longing to see the Lord — the longing felt by the
whole people of God but embodied here in Simeon. Ps 14:7

And then in walked a young woman carrying what seemed to be an ordinary baby, and the Holy Spirit sang within him. His heart burst with the joy of seeing his Savior. Every moment, every ache, every tear was worth the rapture of taking God incarnate in his arms, and Simeon cried out, *Lord, Master, I can die happy now. This is all I've ever wanted. This child is the salvation of the world, the one who will shed light on the Gentiles and bring glory to Israel.* Tears streaming down his face, Simeon realized that this infant Messiah was more than he had ever hoped.

We're not, of course, bound to believe such a legend about Simeon being a centenarian three times over, but there's much to be gained from meditating on his model of a life lived hungry for the Lord. Do we wait for the Lord the way Simeon
did? Do we cry out Maranatha! "Come, Lord Jesus!" and truly Rv 22:20
mean it? Do we rejoice when we encounter him in the Eucharist? Do we see his face in the marginalized, the awkward, the inconvenient? Do we pay him any attention at all?

Simeon's heart leaped when he saw Jesus, and he prophesied that Jesus was the salvation not only of Jews but of Gentiles as well. As we'll see again and again, there was generally very little love lost between Jew and Gentile. After centuries of subjugation, many Jews saw every Gentile as an enemy, a God-forsaken sinner with no hope of pleasing the Lord. Despite the prophets' promise that

Is 25:6–8; 56:3–8; Jer 3:17; Tb 14:6–7; Zec 14:16; Dn 7:14 the Gentiles would one day worship the Lord, despite the covenant with Abraham foretelling that all the nations (another word for Gentiles) would find blessing through his Gn 22:18 descendants, many Jews had no desire for the Gentiles to be blessed in any way. The prophet Jonah had gone so far Jon 1:2–12 as to prefer death over the task of calling the Gentiles to repentance. Indeed, it was Paul's insistence that he had been Acts 22:21–22 sent to bring the Good News to the Gentiles that set him on the path to his death in Rome.

But here Simeon spoke first of revelation to the Gentiles, then of glory for Israel. He referenced two passages from Is 42:6, 49:6 Isaiah that were so pro-Gentile some rabbis were inclined to ignore them entirely. The God who chose a peasant for his mother and sent angels to shepherds was reconciling the 2 Cor 5:19 whole world to himself, Jew and Gentile alike.

As always, the joy of the Incarnation stands in the shadow of the Cross. While Mary and Joseph stood amazed, Simeon blessed them both and then spoke to Mary, as though he knew Joseph would die before these things came to pass. Jesus had come not only to exalt the lowly, Simeon told the young mother, but also to cast down the mighty, to reveal the thoughts of people's hearts. Again and again we see in the Gospels that people become more fully themselves when they encounter Jesus, for good or for ill. They find courage and follow him like the disciples, or they embrace cowardice or cruelty like Herod and Caiaphas. When we truly encounter Christ, when the thoughts of our hearts are revealed, there are only two choices: to follow or to run.

In the midst of all this, Simeon offered a word of warning — and perhaps of consolation — for the Blessed Mother: "You yourself a sword will pierce." He promised that Mary would share in her Son's passion, that she would suffer alongside him. And while his words must have sent a thrill of fear through her, perhaps they also gave her some comfort: Jesus would not suffer alone. She would walk beside him. In the ten months since Gabriel's visit, Mary must have pored over the words of Scripture as they spoke of the Messiah. Her

mind, unclouded by sin, must have understood more than
anyone else had yet, realizing that her son would be pierced Is 53:5;
for our offenses and crushed for our sins. But here she was 1 Pt 2:23–24
given a promise: She would share in his pain; he would not
suffer alone.

Having heard from Simeon, we now meet Anna. Luke has a habit of pairing accounts of men with accounts of women, balancing the two in a way that must have been quite shocking to his ancient readers. It's as if Luke thought women were just as valuable as men — which is, of course, exactly what he thought. Every time we see parallel events or parables with men and women, it's a reminder that Christianity was radical in its promotion of the rights and dignity of women, that Jesus was no misogynist but rather a great lover of women and a champion of their cause.

Here, that's evidenced by Luke's inclusion of an elderly
woman. Anna was of the tribe of Asher, one of the ten tribes
that had been in schism since the reign of Solomon's son. 1 Kgs 12:19
Her presence there spoke to the promise of reunification between the northern and southern kingdoms. Jesus came to Jer 3:11–18
call the faithful of the kingdom of Judah and also those who
had strayed, the pious and the fallen, Jews and Samaritans
and Gentiles. Anna spoke to the universality of his mission
even while he was still in diapers.

Luke tells us that the prophetess Anna never left the
Temple, which indicates that she had likely known Mary
during Mary's youth, which was spent (according to an ancient tradition) in the Temple. But Anna's eyes were fixed
on Jesus, and she spoke not only to the family but also to
all gathered there. Her words haven't come down to us, but
the story of an elderly woman as prophetess and evangelist
should compel us to speak also to all who are awaiting their
redemption — that is, to everybody. We may not, like Simeon and Anna, be privileged to spend all our lives in church
— likely most of us don't even want to, nor should we. We
have other ways of being about our Father's business. But Lk 2:49
we must, like them, find the courage to proclaim the Good

Heb 12:2 News. We must fix our eyes on Jesus, waiting faithfully for the Lord, delighting in his presence, and then making him known to the world. Followers of Jesus can't live with their lips sealed.

Chapter Four

The Childhood of the Christ

11. The Visit of the Magi: Matthew 2:1–12

All this time, a group of Gentiles had been traveling to see the newborn king. We can't know the exact timing of each event, as only Luke writes of the Presentation and only Matthew of the visit of the magi. But since the Holy Family wouldn't have fled to Egypt and then returned to Jerusalem in time for the Presentation, it stands to reason that the magi came to Bethlehem after the Presentation, following a star that heralded the birth of a new King of the Jews.

Scholars can tell us little about the magi, though the word was originally used for Persian priests. There is some speculation that the long-ago magicians who had been Daniel's opponents, and over whom he eventually held authority, Dn 5:29
were the ancestors of the magi. If this is the case, it's possible that for centuries the magi had been passing on the Messianic prophecies of Daniel (along with their timeline). Jews Dn 9:24–27
who stayed behind after the end of the Babylonian Captivity may also have shared their wisdom with the generations of magi who preceded these few, leading them to study other Old Testament texts that pointed to the Christ. This would explain their interest in such a minor event as the birth of a king in a small and subjugated nation — interest so great as

to compel them to follow a star for weeks despite the many dangers. Still, we wonder: What were they seeking? What did they hope to find? Were they driven by mere curiosity, or did their hearts somehow know that they, too, needed to bow before the King of the Jews? Countless astronomical phenomena have been suggested as the possible Star of Bethlehem; what's certain is that the star the magi saw was remarkable enough to send them forth from their homes and into the lair of cruel King Herod the Great, seeking the "king of the Jews."

This title is an interesting one. It's the title used by
Herod, but in the Gospels, only Gentiles ever use it of Jesus,
and (other than the magi) they use it only in connection with
Jn 18:33, 39; the cross. On Good Friday, Jesus was accused of claiming to
19:3, 19, 21 be King of the Jews, abused with the title, and crucified under a placard proclaiming it. Here, again, we see the shadow
of the Cross cast over the Nativity.

When the magi approached Herod to pay homage to the newborn king, they likely assumed they were coming to honor Herod's son. They weren't expecting danger for themselves, nor did they anticipate infanticide. But Herod knew nothing of a newborn king and was, of course, "greatly troubled." All Jerusalem worried, as was only reasonable when Herod became troubled: Herod's insecurity caused heads to roll.

The scholars he consulted likely told him of the Messianic star foretold by Balaam: "A star shall advance from
Nm 24:17 Jacob, / and a scepter shall rise from Israel." Balaam spoke of
the coming Messiah, symbolized by a star. But Herod's concern wasn't just over this portion of the prophecy; Balaam
had gone on to say that the star from Judah would strike at
Nm 24:18 its enemies until "Edom will be dispossessed." Herod, who
was so obsessed with keeping his throne that he had three of
his own sons murdered, was rightly disturbed by this prophecy. He was himself an Edomite, no Jew at all. He held the
throne of Judea by Rome's command, but the Jews chafed
under the rule of a man who wasn't descended even from

Israel, much less David. And now a star was rising, a star that might rob him of his kingdom.

For once, Herod was patient. He continued to gather information before beginning his murderous rampage. Where
did the Scriptures say the Messiah would be born, he asked.
In Bethlehem, the Jewish scholars answered, and sly Herod Mi 5:1
called the magi back in. He made conversation, wondering
how their trip had been, how long they had been on the road,
and when the star had first appeared. Satisfied that he knew
the approximate age of the child he would have to eliminate,
Herod passed along the information about Bethlehem and
made the magi promise to return, "that I too may go and do
him homage."

The wise men continued on their way, traveling only six more miles before the star settled over a house in Bethlehem where the young family was living. Filled with joy, they entered the house and fell on their faces to honor the baby king in humble attire.

It's remarkable enough that they traveled so far to greet a
foreign ruler, still more that they acknowledged him despite
his poverty. But when they prostrated themselves before him,
it became clear that they knew he was more than just the
future king of Israel. These leaders among the Gentiles laid
out gifts far exceeding what even a king would warrant. The
gold was a natural enough gift to a young king, but incense
is offered to gods, while myrrh anoints priests or corpses. Ex 30:23–30;
These gifts indicate that they were bowing before a king who Jn 19:39
was both priest and god, a king born to die.

But while we are accustomed to the idea that myrrh
"breathes a life of gathering gloom," the biblical account Ps 45:9;
shows myrrh also as a perfume for lovers. The book that con- Est 2:12;
tains the most references to myrrh says nothing of priests Prv 7:17
or death: It's the Song of Songs, where myrrh is associated
with bride and bridegroom. In fact, the bridegroom-king of
Solomon's love poem is described as "perfumed with myrrh
and frankincense," as was the Christ child. Thus anointed, Song 3:6
he came "like columns of smoke," reminiscent of the smoke

Gn 15:17; that wrought the covenant with Abraham and wreathed Si-
Ex 19:18 nai as a sign of God's presence, that filled the home of Isaiah
Is 6:4; Ez 10:18; and departed from the Temple in the sight of Ezekiel: the
11:23 glory cloud. In bringing myrrh the magi were, perhaps un-
beknownst to themselves, heralding baby Jesus as the divine
Rv 19:7, 21:9 bridegroom of the Church.

This scene calls to mind the prophecy of Isaiah, who
said, "All from Sheba shall come / bearing gold and frankin-
Is 60:6 cense, / and heralding the praises of the LORD." Tobit, too,
Tb 13:11 prophesied that a bright light would shine to all parts of the
earth (both the literal light of the star and the Light of Christ come into the world), drawing the Gentiles to Israel to offer gifts to the king of heaven. From his earliest childhood, Jesus was calling Gentiles to himself, he who had come "to gather into one the dispersed children of God." He was recognized
Ps 72:10–11, 15 (as the psalms foretold) by the leaders of the nations, who
offered gifts and paid him homage. As we meditate on this astonishing scene, in which an impoverished infant is worshipped by foreign sages, we too are called to bow low before the Christ child, offering him the gold of our treasure, the frankincense of our worship, and the myrrh of our sacrifices. And like the magi, we must go away changed.

12. The Flight into Egypt: Matthew 2:13–15

But this foretaste of glory couldn't last. Herod was fuming in his palace, waiting to destroy anyone who would threaten his claim to the throne. Warned by an angel not to return to Herod, the wise men went on their way. But the Holy Family remained. Joseph was a man who moved only on the Lord's direction; if he hadn't been told to flee, he would stand his ground.

That night, though, the call came: "Take the child and his mother, flee to Egypt." We can't imagine what Joseph's
reaction to that order must have been. From the time of Gen-
Gn 26:2 esis, God had repeatedly told his people *not* to go to Egypt.
Ancient Egypt was the great oppressor, the nation that had enslaved the Israelites and taught them to commit idolatry.

Egyptian horses fooled Israel into relying on themselves in- Dt 17:16; Is 31:1
stead of God. Israel's exile at the hands of Assyria was a direct result of their king's insistence that they rely on Egypt, 2 Kgs 17:4, 7
though God himself had set them free from Egypt's power.
Jeremiah begged the people of Judah not to go to Egypt Jer 42:15–16, 19
when threatened with deportation to Babylon. Again and
again God had cried, *Do not go to Egypt!*

For nearly two millennia, God had warned his people of
the dangers of Egypt, this nation that symbolized sin in the
Jewish imagination. The Father longed to protect us, sinners
though we are, but he "did not spare his own Son." And so Rom 8:32
when Jesus entered into the human experience, he took on all
of it, like us in all things but sin. In his journey into Egypt, Heb 4:15
he was united with Israel, who had gone down into Egypt
and been called back out by God. His suffering here, like our Hos 11:1
suffering, has a purpose: both to fulfill the Old Testament
type of Israel's return from the enemy's land and (through Jer 31:16
the symbolism of pagan Egypt) to manifest his willingness
to walk into the most sinful of places, the most sinful of
hearts, to save souls.

The Word of God contains layer upon layer of truth,
and so in the flight into Egypt we see Jesus being protected
from Herod, Jesus fulfilling prophecy, Jesus entering into
our mess, and, as the Fathers tell us, Jesus bringing the light
of his presence into the darkness of pagan Egypt. He went
to destroy the idols of Egypt and to melt the stony hearts
of Israel's ancient enemies. And perhaps there were Egyp- Is 19:1
tians who met the tiny Savior and felt the Spirit move, as
Simeon and Anna had. God willing, we'll meet them in
heaven, these unnamed saints transformed by an encounter
with the homeless Christ child who would stop at nothing
to save them.

13. The Slaughter of the Innocents: Matthew 2:16–18

As God was bringing light into Egypt, the powers of darkness were also at work. Herod, a ruler patterned after the

Pharaoh who had ordered the slaughter of the Israelite babies
Ex 1:22 at Moses' birth, was trying to protect his crown. Though Scripture is silent on the subject, the first-century Jewish historian Josephus relates a contemporary belief that Pharaoh's attempted genocide was prompted by his astrologers, who had reported to him that a Hebrew child was to be born who would liberate the captive Israelites and bring Egypt low. Pharaoh's response was to kill every baby boy among the Israelites. When Herod encountered astrologers telling him that a Jewish boy had been born who would destroy his reign as Moses had destroyed Pharaoh's, he did just as Pharaoh had done.

Every boy child under two was ripped from his mother's arms and slaughtered as she watched. The babies Mary had held, the toddlers who had kissed baby Jesus' sweet forehead, all were collateral damage in Herod's quest to rule. The streets of Bethlehem ran red with blood.

All the while, Mary and Joseph were rushing through the darkness to save their skins, abandoning their friends to the mercies of Herod the Filicide. They were refugees, fleeing to a country where they knew nobody, impoverished migrants desperately trying to learn the language while Joseph looked for work. During their sojourn in Egypt, perhaps their dreams were haunted by the echoes of Bethlehem's screams. Perhaps they thought back to Bethlehem, to their grieving friends who mourned the loss of the children they would never know had died as martyrs. Maybe Holy Mary and Good Saint Joseph cried out to God, demanding to know why he hadn't stopped the slaughter.

Like us, Mary and Joseph knew well that being in God's will doesn't always make life easy or pleasant. They knew that God doesn't answer every prayer. Still, he is good. And when their grief and their guilt threatened to rob them of that conviction, they clung to Jesus and let his love ease their pain. We who weep and mourn and rage against the Lord can take comfort in that image: holding tight to the Christ child while we weep over our loss.

14. The Return from Egypt: *Matthew 2:19–23*; Luke 2:39–40

We don't know how long the Holy Family spent in Egypt. Months, perhaps a year or two. Not long enough to feel settled in a land so foreign. Not long enough to get over the terror Herod's threat had inspired in them. No, they waited and wondered and likely worried until the death of Herod the Great (and another angelic message) set them moving again. Joseph was visited by another angel, again in a dream. Joseph the carpenter had joined Joseph the dreamer of dreams in saving his family by going to Egypt. Now it was time to return, (Gn 37—46) and Joseph was as obedient as ever. He knew the Messiah was to be from Bethlehem, so to Bethlehem he planned to (Mi 5:1) return. But news of the political situation changed his mind.

It's unlikely that Herod the Great had shared the motive for his attack on the babies of Bethlehem with anybody; any whisper of Balaam's prophecy being fulfilled would (Nm 24:17–18) have undermined his claim to the throne. Still, when Joseph learned that Judea was being ruled by Herod the Great's son Herod Archelaus (who had begun his reign by murdering three thousand Jews in the Temple), Joseph led the family to the even smaller town of Nazareth in out-of-the-way Galilee. Surely there his son — God's Son — would be safe.

The Messiah had to be born in Bethlehem, but the quotation Matthew offers here about Nazareth is a curious one. Nowhere in the Old Testament does it explicitly say, "He shall be called a Nazorean." Matthew would have known this, but he's unconcerned. It seems his intention isn't to offer a direct quotation but to refer to the Old Testament idea of the Messianic *branch*, *netser* in Hebrew. Isaiah speaks of the branch (*netser*) that would spring from the stump of Jesse, (Is 11:1) the father of King David. Later prophets elaborated on this idea, though they used a different term. Jeremiah spoke of a shoot or branch being raised up to David, while Zechariah (Jer 23:5; 33:14–16) promised that a branch would come and rebuild the Temple. (Zec 3:8; 6:12) Interestingly, the Septuagint translates *branch* in these passages as *dawn* or *daybreak* — the same word used to refer to

Lk 1:78 the coming Messiah in Zechariah's canticle. Matthew sees God's Providence at work in Jesus' birth in Bethlehem, in his flight into Egypt, and in his childhood in Nazareth. None of this is wasted, none an accident. Likely Mary and Joseph, too, were able to look at their tumultuous lives — so different from what they'd expected — and choose to see the hand of God bringing good out of all the evil. Because even when we can't see it, God is always at work.

15. The Finding of the Child Jesus at the Temple: Luke 2:41–52

At this, the Gospels leave the Holy Family for nearly thirty years. With only one exception, the hidden life at Nazareth is shrouded in silence. We know only that Jesus "grew and became strong, filled with wisdom; and the favor of God was upon him." But we can't skim past those years just because the Gospels do. There is much to be gained from imagining how Jesus, Mary, and Joseph may have interacted with each other, what Joseph's workday may have looked like, or how he might have broken his scriptural silence to joke with his wife. We can wonder about how Mary dealt with the neighborhood gossip or how she mothered all the children and adults in the town. We can smile over their tenderness as a family and strive to love as they did. We can meditate on this carpenter's son, who daily heard the echo of the nails that would bind him to his death, and think again: *For me. All for me.*

Still, but for one visit to Jerusalem, all we can do is imagine. The only light the evangelists shed on those thirty years is a confusing scene when Jesus was twelve. Each year the family went up to Jerusalem for Passover, as they likely did for Pentecost and the feast of Tabernacles, the other two pil-
Dt 16:16; Tb 1:6 grim feasts of Israel. Though only Joseph would have been required to go, Jesus and Mary were eager to pray at the Temple, the beating heart of Judaism, and likely eager as well to visit with family and friends in the festival atmosphere. When Jesus was nearly a man, his mother and father gave him some freedom, trusting him to remain with the caravan.

They must have been horrified when they realized that he wasn't there. They had already traveled a day's journey from Jerusalem before even realizing that they had lost the Son of God. Panic rising in their hearts, they ran from group to group, demanding to know if anyone had seen him.

This wasn't like him. Jesus had always been such an obedient son. But now, on the brink of manhood, he was reminding them whose Son he truly was. When it became apparent that he hadn't joined the caravan in the first place, Joseph and Mary hurried back to Jerusalem, hoping against hope that nothing terrible had happened.

They found him in the Temple area, surrounded by scholars who were astounded at his understanding. This word *astounded* (which some translations render "amazed") is such a powerful adjective that this passage might well be translated, "All who heard him were *beside themselves* at his understanding." Indeed, one of the other times it's used in the Gospels is when the crowds accused Jesus of being out of his mind. Here, Jesus' listeners stood before him with Mk 3:21
mouths agape, nearly out of their minds with awe at the wisdom of this boy who wasn't even old enough to grow a beard.

When Mary and Joseph happened upon the scene (or, rather, rushed frantically upon the scene), they, too, were astonished — or bewildered, as some translations render it, since this was a very different reaction from that of the scholars. It wasn't Jesus' wisdom that shocked them; they had become accustomed to that. There was radiant joy at finding him safe and well in this foretaste of the Resurrection. But there was also distress at finding him casually teaching the elders as though his beloved parents hadn't been frantic with worry. Even the sinless Mother of God responded with great emotion here, reminding us that our feelings are not sins: "Son, why have you done this to us?" There was anxiety and pain in her voice, though perhaps not rebuke. As the mother of the divine one, Mary had spent twelve years learning that while she was his mother, he was her Lord. "Your father and I have been looking for you with great anxiety." She may have wanted to correct, but she certainly wanted to understand. What had he been trying to teach her?

Finally, we have the first recorded words of Jesus, words we would do well to ask ourselves: "Why were you looking for me?" Jesus asks us all this question, both about the hunger in our hearts that first drove us to seek him and about the reason we are trying to know him better now. What longing
Rv 2:4 once led us to that love we had at first? Has it faded now? Are we looking to Jesus as King and Savior or merely as a source of comfort and stability? Do we seek platitudes or are we searching for truth, however uncomfortable? Have we made Jesus the Lord of our entire lives, or are there some areas we prefer to control ourselves?

For Mary, the question was more pointed. He sounds almost hurt, his question echoed by the one he would pose to Philip twenty years later: "Have I been with you for so long
Jn 14:9 a time and you still do not know me?" This time, the boy Jesus was speaking to one who ought to have known better even than his apostles: *Why didn't you know where you would find me? Where else would I be? You tell me my father was looking for me. Have you forgotten who my Father truly is? I had to be in my Father's house.* The Greek could also be translated "about my Father's business." Jesus had been perfectly obedient to his parents for his whole life, but soon he would be a man and his true Father would ask things of him that would call him out of their home. In this painful episode, he was reminding them that he belonged to the Father above all.

Though his entire hidden life at Nazareth is summarized here with he "was obedient to them," this incident reminded Mary and Joseph of who Jesus was. He was not theirs to control, nor would he always be able to submit to their will. He would one day have to begin making his way to Calvary. Still, in being found on the third day, Jesus was pointing toward his Resurrection. Though he would go forth from Mary's side to die in obedience to his Father, on the third day he would rise. Twenty years later — at another Passover — this pain and loss and reunion would be repeated, the suffering far greater and the joy beyond compare.

Mary didn't understand these things yet, but she kept them in her heart, continuing to learn how to let Jesus be God as he advanced in wisdom and age and favor. What a gift that we can look to her, sinless but still uncertain, as we seek to navigate a life in which the God we love so often fails to act as we expect, in which he seems even to have abandoned us, leaving us frantically searching for him and demanding, "Why have you done this to us?" Mary's example teaches us how to seek him even when he seems distant. It teaches us to trust that he is working even then. And it gives us permission to cry out in our fear and anxiety, to bring him our confused and hurting hearts, and to try to trust, pondering these things in our hearts even when we do not understand.

Chapter Five

John the Baptist Prepares the Way

16. John the Baptist: Matthew 3:1–12; Mark 1:2–8; *Luke 3:1–20*; John 1:19–28

With that, we've suddenly reached Jesus' adulthood. We see nothing of the friendships he formed in Nazareth, the wisdom he shared with his neighbors, the work he did in his carpenter's shop. We can only imagine the death of Joseph — with Mary on one side and Jesus on the other — and ask Joseph's intercession for a happy death ourselves. We don't see Jesus learning to walk or to read or to carve. We can't trace the scars on his knees or the smile lines around his eyes. We don't truly know what shade of skin he had or what texture of hair. We who seek to fix our eyes on Jesus know so little.

But finally, with the ministry of John the Baptist beginning in the desert, we begin to see what sort of man Jesus was. We will watch him cast down the mighty and lift up
the lowly. We will wonder why he weeps and why he sleeps Lk 1:52
and why he shouts. This essential work of gazing at Jesus will bear fruit only by the power of the Holy Spirit at work through his Word. May our hearts be opened to know him as we are known.

First, though, the forerunner. Luke has told us of John the Baptist, the priestly son of Elizabeth and Zechariah and cousin to Jesus, the man consecrated before his birth and set apart as a prophet. Now we see him in action, clothed
2 Kgs 1:8 in camel's hair reminiscent of Elijah's and living on locusts and honey, the wild prophet of the desert calling the people of God to conversion: "Repent, for the kingdom of heaven is at hand!"

John's ministry was the beginning of Jesus' ministry, so Luke takes great care to situate us within history. He names the emperor, the governor, all three tetrarchs, and the high priests — both because he is a historian and because this ministry of Jesus is the turning point of human history. Everything that had come to pass up to that point was a mere prologue to the drama about to unfold. The events Luke is about to recount would impact not just Jerusalem and Judea, but Rome and all the world, down through the ages, even until the end of time. John's journey through the desert inviting people to repentance sounded the death knell for Satan's rule, and Luke wants to be very sure that we understand it as a real historical event, not some myth or fantasy.

At first John must have seemed little more than a lone fanatic, but Luke describes him quite clearly as a prophet. He tells us, "The word of God came to John," reminiscent of the formula used in reference to Elijah and Samuel and Jonah, used twenty-one times in the Book of Jeremiah and fifty times in Ezekiel. If John was speaking as these great prophets had, it's no surprise that before long thousands of people were making the trip out to be baptized.

When Matthew and Mark tell us that "all the inhabitants of Jerusalem were going out to him," that may not be much of an exaggeration. God had been silent for centuries, with no prophets arising since shortly after the Jews had returned from exile in the fifth century BC. For centuries, all through the rule of Greece and Egypt and Syria and Rome, there had been nobody speaking the word of the Lord to his people. As Amos had foretold, there was "Not a hunger for

bread, or a thirst for water, / but for hearing the word of the
Lord." Then suddenly, John the Baptist appeared, dressed as Am 8:11
Elijah and calling the people out into the desert to descend
into the Jordan and then to reenter the Promised Land set
free from their captivity to sin — a new beginning for the
descendants of those who had crossed the Jordan to enter the
Promised Land centuries before. The writings of the proph- Jos 3:14–17
ets had ended with a promise that one would come in the
spirit of Elijah to herald the coming of the day of the Lord. Mal 3:23
Here John began where Malachi left off, as though centuries hadn't intervened: Elijah had returned, and the Lord was
coming.

In the eyes of the Jews who had bowed their heads under
foreign rule for centuries, the Babylonian Captivity had never truly ended. They were still in exile, with no Davidic king
to lead them. Though we might expect them to have chafed
under the accusations of the Baptist as he demanded that
they repent, they had been longing for some prophet to arise
and tell them what they must do to regain God's favor. "Oh,
that from Zion might come / the salvation of Israel!" they
prayed with the psalmist. "Jacob would rejoice, and Israel
be glad / when the Lord. restores his people!" They had lost Ps 14:7
the Promised Land through sin; now, the prophet foretold by
Isaiah was crying out in the desert and showing them how to Is 40:3–5
prepare a highway for their God. This was the beginning of Bar 5:7
their vindication!

Indeed, the Baptist himself claimed these words of Isaiah when the priests and Levites asked him who he was, as
John describes in his Gospel: "I am 'the voice of one crying
out in the desert, / "Make straight the way of the Lord."'" Is 40:3
Though Mark's Gospel regularly recounts Jesus quoting
the Old Testament, there's only one time that Mark himself
quotes the Old Testament, and it's the very beginning of his
Gospel, when he anchors us in the ancient prophecies that
pointed to John the Baptist. For Mark, whose Gospel is so Mal 3:1; Is 40:3
urgently action-driven that he uses the word *immediately* for-
ty-one times in sixteen chapters, it takes a prophecy of great

significance to make him pause in his storytelling to recite it.

This passage comes to us from the beginning of the second half of Isaiah, called "the book of consolation." After
thirty-nine chapters of prophesying woe, Isaiah had been
called to speak comfort instead: "Comfort, give comfort to
my people, / says your God. / Speak to the heart of Jerusalem, and proclaim to her / that her service is ended, / that
Is 40:1–2 her guilt is expiated." When John cried out in the desert, it
was the beginning of Israel's freedom and the salvation of
the world. Later in the same chapter, Isaiah proclaimed this
good news (translated *euangelion* in the Septuagint): "Here
Is 40:9 is your God!"

John the Baptist's claim, then, was more than that of a
typical prophet. He was declaring himself the one who proclaims the Gospel that God is with us, the Good Shepherd
Is 40:11 promised by Isaiah. Something new was happening here —
something terrifying and exciting. Something that offered a
hope Israel hadn't known in centuries.

So they streamed out to the Jordan, the river the Israelites
Jos 3:14–17; had crossed to enter the Promised Land, the site of deliver-
2 Kgs 5 ance and miraculous healing in days of old. In this moment
of grace, they took their eyes off their neighbors' failings and
acknowledged their own sins instead. They plunged into the
Jordan, baptized in a new ritual that had its roots in the rit-
Lv 14:8 ual cleansings of the Old Testament but was more: a turning
point in the lives of those who received it rather than a mere
return to ritual purity.

John's response to the repenting crowds wasn't exactly congratulatory. He railed against their sin. "You brood of vipers!" he cried, though Matthew indicates that he was primarily addressing the Pharisees and Sadducees with these words. "Produce good fruits as evidence of your repentance. And do not presume to say to yourselves, 'We have Abraham as our father.'"

We would do well at this point to take a moment to familiarize ourselves with the major factions at play here, notably the Pharisees, the scribes, and the Sadducees. While the word *Pharisee* has become synonymous with "legalistic hypocrite," the movement itself had many merits, and Pharisees were generally very well-respected by the people — so much so that years after his conversion, Paul still held up his status as a Pharisee as a point of pride. (Acts 23:6; 26:5; Phil 3:5) In the years after the Maccabean revolt, priests had taken on secular as well as religious authority, leaving them open to even more corruption than before. The Pharisees had arisen in opposition to the lax observance of God's law, seeking to study the law and observe it exactly. The oral traditions they developed arose from their study of the Torah and are the foundation of rabbinic Judaism today. As a group, they worked to preserve Jewish law and customs in the face of increased contact with Gentiles, desiring above all to be pleasing to God by obedience to his law. The surplus of rules that resulted weren't in themselves problematic (as Jesus himself acknowledged), (Lk 11:42; Mt 23:3) though modern Christians often associate any rules at all with the alleged sin of "pharisaism." But this movement wasn't about control and rigor; it was an attempt to live righteously in covenant relationship with the God who had called his people out of Egypt and formed them to be his own. To their contemporaries, the Pharisees were the equivalent of our daily communicants, our full-time missionaries, our church employees with degrees in theology. They were the most faithful, the ones everyone else looked at in wonder because of their dedication to their faith.

But men are fallen, and Pharisees were sometimes (perhaps often) more concerned with the letter of the law than with its spirit. They demanded exacting obedience from everyone in order to earn God's favor, despite the repeated Old Testament assurances that God's love for Israel persists whatever their sins. (Ez 16; Hosea; Is 54:10) Some, like Nicodemus, were genuinely seeking God through their pursuit of righteousness; when they saw Jesus, they recognized him. (Jn 3:1–15; 19:39–42) Others had made an idol of the law and saw the Christ only as a transgressor. We who stand in the same place — the Bible study leaders, the parish council members, the ones praying the Rosary on our knees — are often inclined to do the same thing: to make our religiosity our God rather than letting our religious practice draw us to God's heart as intended. If we fail to see ourselves in the Pharisees rebuked by John and Jesus, we've missed the whole point.

Many of the scribes were Pharisees as well, though not
Acts 23:9 all. They were legal scholars, experts in the requirements not
only of the Mosaic law but also of those accumulated tradi-
Mk 7:8; tions of men that Jesus cautioned against putting in the place
Mt 15:1–6 of God. To be a scribe was a profession; they made their liv-
ing by writing out contracts and consulting on legal issues,
while most Pharisees seem to have worked at jobs that were
Acts 18:3 unrelated to the law. Scribes would have been well-educated,
likely very familiar not only with the law (the first five books
of the Bible) but with the Word of God more broadly. Again,
Mt 8:19; many were Godly men, but others were smug or legalistic or
Mk 12:28–34 hypocritical — fallen in the way so many of us are fallen.
To point out their need for continued conversion, Jesus oc-
Mt 19:4; casionally replied to their challenges with subtle criticisms of
Jn 5:39–40 their scholarship.

Sadducees, on the other hand, seem to have had less to recommend them. Though many of them were priests, they were more concerned with being aristocrats than with anything else. Some may have been serious about their religious practice, but (unlike the Pharisees) that was the exception rather than the rule. They were the merchants and rulers of Judah, the elite class that had compromised with the pagans in order to maintain their power and their lives of luxury. Unlike the Pharisees, they rejected the traditions that had arisen around the Torah and even rejected the other books in the Tanakh (the Hebrew Scriptures), holding only the Pentateuch to be canonical. This led to their disbelief in the resur-
Mt 22:23–33 rection of the dead, over which they would clash with Jesus.
The Pharisees, meanwhile, joined their more recent ances-
2 Mc 7:11, 14 tors, the Maccabees, in believing that there was some sort of
resurrection, though they were uncertain as to the details.

John was unconcerned with the Sadducees' pedigrees and the Pharisees' CVs. Indeed, he was adamant that even bap-

tism wasn't enough. His baptism (unlike the baptism commanded by Jesus) was only a symbol of conversion. Those Mt 28:19–20;
who were baptized had to live differently. They couldn't call 1 Pt 3:21
on the name of Abraham and brandish their Jewish blood Mt 3:9
while defrauding the poor and defying the law. Conversion
isn't just a matter of belief, the emotional response of a fren-
zied crowd before a charismatic preacher. No, true conversion involves a change of life. And the consequences, John
assured them, would be grave if Israel's leaders failed to act:
"Even now the ax lies at the root of the trees." In the face
of their disbelief, Jesus later cursed a fig tree, the symbol of
Israel, and caused it to wither in confirmation of John's dire Hos 9:10; Jer 24
prediction. This was no empty threat. Mt 21:19–20

Such was the power of the Spirit at work within John
that, when they were thus excoriated, the people didn't attack him or turn away. They responded eagerly, "What then
should we do?" a question that would later be echoed by
those who heard Peter preach on the day of Pentecost. The Acts 2:37
Baptist's answer wasn't another hundred commandments
added to the 613 already found in the Old Testament. It
wasn't minutiae about specific Sabbath observances, as was
the Pharisees' wont. It was simple: "Whoever has two tunics
should share with the person who has none. And whoever
has food should do likewise."

Even tax collectors were repenting — those traitors who
colluded with the enemy, were ritually impure, and exploited
their countrymen. Rabbinic texts treated them as sinners
who were unlikely to repent, but there they were, listening
to the preaching of John. When they asked him what they
should do, John didn't demand that they repay everything
they'd ever stolen, as we'll see the love of Jesus later prompted
Zacchaeus to do. He didn't tell them to quit their jobs out- Lk 19:8
right. Instead, he moved them slowly toward true conversion: "Stop collecting more than what is prescribed." The
forerunner left it there — let the Divine Physician effect the
complete cure.

Stunning as the conversion of multiple tax collectors

must have been, it was nothing to the sight that Luke casually mentions next: Soldiers asked the same question. "And what is it that we should do?" In first-century Palestine, they were almost certainly Roman soldiers, pagan representatives of the oppressive overlords who had driven the Jews nearly to despair. They, too, were seeking righteousness. They, too, were called to salvation. Again, John was gentle, not demanding that they be circumcised or abandon their soldiering. He asked them merely to be decent. "Do not practice extortion, do not falsely accuse anyone, and be satisfied with your wages." For pagans and tax collectors, the bar was set low — for the time being. John was merely preparing the way for the one who would say, "Be perfect, just as your
Mt 5:48 heavenly Father is perfect." With scribes and Pharisees, those men who had been given much, who were convinced of their own righteousness, John felt less of a need to be gentle.

As the crowds stood before this man who preached with power, who spoke truth with little concern for the consequences, who looked like a prophet and spoke like a prophet, they asked themselves, *Could he possibly be the Prophet?* Not just *a* prophet, wondrous as even that was, but *the* prophet
Dt 18:15 foretold by Moses, the new Moses who was to come. Could he be the Messiah, the long-awaited Son of David? Overcome by curiosity, some priests and Levites came from Jerusalem to ask, "Who are you?"

John knew exactly what they were asking, and though he could easily have gotten the crowds to follow him, he remembered who he was and spoke the truth: "I am not the Messiah." Nor was he Elijah, whose return to herald the
Mal 3:23; Messiah had been foretold, nor the Prophet to whom God's
Dt 18:15 people would listen. He was the prologue, he told them, to grab their attention before the Logos arrived.

"I am not worthy to loosen the thongs of his sandals," he proclaimed. Who then, would the Messiah be? Removing a man's sandal was considered a task so menial and degrading that only a slave could be asked to perform it — a custom that was well-established by the time of the third-century

rabbi Yehoshua ben Levi, as attested in paragraph 96a of the Ketubot tractate of the Talmud. But John said he wasn't worthy to do such a thing. If the one to come was so great that the world's first prophet in 500 years was lower than a slave before him, he would be more than a prophet, more even than merely a Messiah. And where John baptized for repentance, a symbol of a desire for conversion, the one coming after him (who, though he was younger than John, out-
ranked him "because he existed before me") would baptize Jn 1:15
with the Holy Spirit and fire. Jesus' baptism would be one of total transformation, one that set a person aflame with God's Spirit.

17. The Baptism of Jesus: *Matthew 3:13–17*; Mark 1:9–11; Luke 3:21–22; John 1:29–34

Into this atmosphere walked an unknown carpenter. As the crowds pushed and shouted and shushed one another, Jesus walked past them all, straight up to his cousin. He was, as
Luke tells us, about thirty. This was a significant age for the Lk 3:23
Jewish people: the age at which Joseph came to power in Egypt Gn 41:46
(saving the world through life-giving grain); the age at which Gn 41:57
King Saul began his disastrous reign and David his illustrious 1 Sm 13:1
one; the age at which Levites originally began their minis- 2 Sm 5:4
try. Jesus had come of age as savior, king, and priest, and Nm 4:2–3
now he was approaching John to be anointed by the Spirit and sent out to save his people.

When Jesus first approached, John was probably delighted. All his life and all his ministry had been preparing for this moment, when he could pass the baton to the true Messiah and take his place at Jesus' right hand. There must have been joy and relief in his eyes as he greeted his beloved cousin.

One wonders if John had realized exactly who Jesus was before that point. Surely his mother would have told him the story of Jesus' conception. He must have known that Jesus was the Messiah — why hide it from him? But when he cried out, "Behold, the Lamb of God, who takes away the sin of

the world," was he as surprised as anyone to hear this man
Rv 5:12 identified as the one who would be sacrificed? To a Jew, the
language "Lamb of God" could only mean one who would
be offered as a holocaust to the Lord. When God had sent
Abraham to sacrifice his only-begotten son, Isaac had asked
Gn 22:7 his father, "Where is the sheep for the burnt offering?" After
God had spared Isaac's life, he provided a ram for sacrifice,
Gn 22:13 but no lamb. Here, John answered Isaac's question: "Behold,
the Lamb of God."

Many years after the sacrifice of Isaac, the Israelites
would again be saved by the sacrifice of a lamb, the unblem-
Ex 12:3–8; ished Paschal lamb by whose blood they were marked in
1 Pt 1:18–19 order to be saved from death. This, too, would have been
evoked by the language "Lamb of God." This is the first time
the Gospels tell us that Jesus would save his people by dying
for them, though the crowds couldn't have understood it at
the time. Was it news to John as well?

The family reunion was further complicated by Jesus' indication that he had come to be baptized. No, no, this John couldn't stomach. He was happy to eat locusts and live in the desert, but to presume to baptize the sinless one? It was too much. "I need to be baptized by you, and yet you are coming to me?" It's the same question we all ask when we read of Jesus' baptism — possibly the same reason that Mark, Luke, and John gloss over the event. If Jesus was without sin and Baptism is a removal of sin, why on earth should he be baptized? If he was the Messiah and John merely the forerunner, why submit to John?

Jesus didn't explain why he chose to be baptized. He just asked for obedience: "Allow it now." For John, this was enough. And the maker of the waters stepped into the Jordan to sanctify all water. In his first public act, Jesus united himself to all sinners, descending into death and rising again, promising the cross and Resurrection from the moment he appeared on the scene.

As Jesus rose up out of the waters, the heavens were torn open, just as the veil that separated God from his people

would be torn from top to bottom at the death of Christ. Isa- Mk 15:38
iah had begged the Lord, "Oh, that you would rend the heavens and come down," and here he did, the Spirit descending Is 63:19
upon Jesus like a dove. The Spirit moved over the face of the
waters as he had at the creation of the world, telling us that Gn 1:2
this baptism was the beginning of the world's recreation. In
taking the form of a dove, he reminded his people of the dove
that led Noah out of the ark into the new world that had Gn 8:8–12
been washed clean of sin.

Perhaps most importantly, the Spirit here descending
on Jesus was anointing him as the Messiah — the Anointed Acts 10:38
One — in the presence of all the people. As the Spirit rested Is 11:2
on the Son, the Father spoke. Here we see the Father, the
Son, and the Holy Spirit, distinct but not separate: the first
true revelation of the Trinity.

The Father looked at his Son and cried out, "This is
my beloved Son, with whom I am well pleased." His words
were an echo of one of Isaiah's servant songs, in which the Is 42:1–7
prophet promised that the Messiah would be gentle and just,
bringing healing and liberation and becoming a light for the
nations, as Simeon had also foretold. Matthew would later Lk 2:32
quote this same passage in reference to Jesus, likely remem- Mt 12:15–21
bering the words that had shaken the hearts of all those who
had found themselves at the Jordan that day.

This divine proclamation was reminiscent also of a
psalm sung at the coronation of Israel's kings: The Lord
"said to me, 'You are my son; / today I have begotten you.'" Ps 2:7
Here, too, there is a shadow of the cross: Five verses earlier
the psalmist had told of the princes of the people conspiring
against God and his anointed, as they would conspire against Ps 2:2
the one now anointed by the Spirit. But the focus of this moment is on the love of the Father, who called Jesus not just his
Son, but his beloved Son — the words used to describe Isaac
as Abraham was taking him to Mount Moriah to sacrifice
him. Jesus was shown to be the new Isaac, the only-begotten Gn 22:2
Son of the Father; in retrospect, we can see his climb to Calvary written all over Isaac's journey up Mount Moriah as he

Gn 22:6 carried the wood for his sacrifice. As the crowds looked on,
Jesus was anointed Messiah and King and declared son of
Abraham and Son of God. In descending into death with us,
he also foretold his own death and resurrection, which would
Is 25:7 destroy the veil that separated us from God.

The Father's delight in his Son couldn't have been new information to Jesus, the Word Incarnate. Still, even those who are most confident in their father's love may find that a thrill runs through them when they hear his pride in them powerfully expressed. Pondering Jesus' joy at the Father's words invites us to ask the Father to do the same for us: to declare himself well pleased in us. There may have been times in our lives, after a particularly difficult confession or at a moment when we made a dramatic choice for the Lord, when we felt his pleasure. But to be rooted in God's love for us, sometimes we need to ask him to speak this truth to our hearts. As we meditate on Jesus' baptism, let's ask the Lord to fill us, at least for a moment, with a certainty of his fierce and tender love.

The Synoptic accounts end with this beautiful moment of divine intimacy, but John tells us more about the Baptist's reaction to the scene. His claim "I did not know him" certainly indicates that some part of this was a surprise to him. Perhaps he didn't recognize his cousin after so many years apart. Perhaps he just didn't realize that the one he was preparing the way for was the same little boy he'd played with during Passover visits to Jerusalem. Or maybe he's speaking in a stunned voice: *I knew he was the Messiah, but I didn't know it would be like this. All these years, I knew he was good, but the very Son of God? I didn't know him. I never really knew him.* And yet, despite what he had thought, John had the clarity to proclaim: "He is the Son of God." John took his place in history as the first human being to speak this truth, having heard it from the very mouth of the Father.

Chapter Six

The Beginning of the Public Ministry

18. The Temptation of Jesus: *Matthew 4:1–11*; Mark 1:12–13; Luke 4:1–13

"At once," Mark tells us, "the Spirit drove him out into the desert." This is an abrupt turn of events. Rather than celebrating his anointing and the announcement of his divine sonship, Jesus retreated into the desert to fast and pray in peace, resting before the beginning of his real work.

Or at least, that's how it seems when we think of fasting and prayer as passive. The testimony of Scripture, though, is that life in the Spirit is one of warfare against the evil one. Jesus had been anointed king at his baptism; like any good king, he was eager to protect his people, which often means waging war on their enemies. So the Spirit thrust him into the desert, traditionally viewed as the domain of Satan, where Jesus grabbed the attention of the devil by showing his faithfulness to the Father.

In the pattern of Moses of old, the new Moses fasted in Ex 34:28
the desert. For forty days and forty nights, Jesus ate nothing. God's son Israel had wandered in the desert for forty Ex 4:22
years, grumbling against God; God's only-begotten Son Jos 5:6
now made himself as weak as he could possibly be and then

triumphed over temptation, redeeming Israel's desert sin.

We can't know what exactly Satan knew about Jesus up
to this point. Though he knows more than any human being, he is not omniscient and might not have been privy to
the Annunciation or even the angels' song at the Nativity.
Even if he had been aware of all that had happened, he might
not have been certain that Jesus truly was God incarnate.
His temptations here seem geared toward determining what
exactly the Baptist meant when he said, "He is the Son of
Jn 1:34 God."

To our ears, "Son of God" is clearly a title of divinity,
interchangeable with "God the Son." We struggle to understand what could possibly be ambiguous about the Father's
proclamation, "This is my beloved Son," or the Baptist's testimony, "This is the Son of God." But to the Jews of Jesus'
day, the "son of God" wasn't an unfamiliar concept. God
Ex 4:22 had declared to Pharaoh that Israel was his son; this language
Hos 11:1 was echoed in Hosea. The king was considered the son of
Ps 2:7 God, and the righteous might even describe themselves as
Wis 2:13 sons of God. None of this meant any more than that they
had been chosen by God. As Jesus' ministry progressed, it
became clear that he had far more in mind when he called
God his Father, but at this point, nobody could be sure what
Jn 14:30 was meant by the phrase, not even the "ruler of the world."

And so the devil tested him — and Jesus allowed it,
redeeming even temptation itself in the process. Each exchange between Jesus and Satan is reminiscent of a failure
Ex 16 of the Israelites in the desert. Jesus was hungry as they were
hungry, but their hunger drove them to complain against
God. Jesus was invited to test God, but the Israelites needed
Ex 17 no invitation. Jesus was asked to bow down before a false
god; the Israelites did just that in the moments after God had
Ex 32 espoused them to himself with the gift of the law. Jesus responded to each temptation with a quotation from the Book
of Deuteronomy, the book of the law given to the Israelites at
the end of their sojourn in the desert.

The devil began by looking at a hungry man and suggesting that he eat. "If you are the Son of God," he challenged, "command that these stones become loaves of bread." It's interesting to note that his first temptation was subtle — there's nothing sinful about a hungry man eating. Nor was Jesus obligated to avoid using his powers for himself, though every one of his recorded miracles was for the benefit of others. Jesus refused, not because miraculously producing food was evil in itself, but because we must never act at Satan's prompting, even to do what seems to be good. Later Jesus would multiply bread and turn bread into his body, but here he would not make even one roll at the prompting of the evil one.

Mk 6:34–44
Mk 14:22–26

Though the most innocuous of the three temptations, this was likely the most difficult to resist. Satan would go on to suggest that Jesus demand things of the Father and that he worship the evil one. Nothing in the heart of Christ desired either of those things. This, the temptation of a starving human being to eat something, was much more attractive. But Jesus, who had entered into our temptation in order to redeem it, would not compromise. He acted only at the Father's prompting, not at the devil's. When Satan offered him pleasure, he responded: *I'd rather be hungry*. He replied in confidence, deeply rooted in the love of the Father. It's worth imagining how we would respond in the same situation; perhaps we would remain strong, but would our resistance be drenched in bitterness? Driven by pride? Haunted by fear? What would need to change in our hearts for our response to temptation to be peaceful and self-assured, as Jesus' was?

When Jesus didn't (or perhaps, in Satan's mind, couldn't) turn stones into bread, the enemy tried again. Matthew and Luke disagree about the order of the next two temptations. In Luke's account, Satan appealed to the human desire for pleasure, then power, then the ultimate: pride. As Matthew frames it, Satan's final attempt was his most ridiculous, asking the Son of God to worship him. In Matthew's account, the devil next took Jesus to the parapet of the Temple. "If you are the Son of God," he wheedled, "throw yourself down." This time, there was no suggestion that Jesus could work some miracle to save himself. Satan wondered if the Father would show his hand by interceding to rescue his falling Son. Jesus had quoted Scripture in response to Satan's first attempted trap, so Satan did the same, adjusting his tactics to the one being tempted (as is his wont).

But the devil likes to quote Scripture out of context, and
he seems to have forgotten the verse that followed his selec-
tion: "You can tread upon the asp and the viper, / trample
Ps 91:13 the lion and the dragon." The one who penned the psalms
must have continued his recitation where the evil one left
off, with this promise that the new Adam would strike at
Gn 3:15 the serpent's head. We may be forgiven for hoping the Lord
quoted it aloud, striking fear in the heart of the one so soon
to be crushed.

This temptation, too, was not to something inherently
evil. But unlike Israel, Jesus was unwilling to demand anything of the Father. "You shall not put the Lord, your God,
Dt 6:16 to the test," he quoted.

Finally, Satan felt he'd taken Jesus' measure. He couldn't
turn stones into bread — it didn't occur to the devil that this
weak, hungry man might be stronger than his temptation —
and he couldn't be sure that angels would catch him when he
fell. *This man might be the Messiah,* Satan must have thought,
but he isn't divine. So the devil made the most alluring offer
he could think of: *I will make you ruler over all the kingdoms
of the earth. If you worship me, you can skip all the difficulties
that await you as Messiah and take this shortcut to success.* For
many of us, it would be quite alluring: glory without the
cross. But asking God the Son to worship a creature is almost
laughable, whatever may be offered in return. Indeed, the
devil looked at the true ruler of the earth and tried to sell
him what was already his own. Even had he been a mere hu-
Ps 72:10–11; man Messiah, it had been prophesied that he would rule over
Dn 7:14 all nations, without the help of Satan. As God himself, he
needed neither military victories nor diabolical intervention
to establish him as King of kings.

Jesus' patience had worn thin, and this suggested blasphemy was the last straw: "Get away, Satan!" he cried, overcoming the devil not with his divine power but with his human will. At that, the devil left him until an opportune time. The reader knows that this battle wasn't over yet. It wouldn't be until Satan thought he had won.

Meanwhile, angels came to minister to Jesus — the same ones Satan had suggested would catch him if he threw himself off the parapet of the Temple. The sinless one lived as we might have: at peace with the wild beasts and served Is 11:6–8
by the angels. He was the New Adam who triumphed where the first Adam fell. By his refusal to succumb to the devil's wiles, we are likewise strengthened in the face of temptation.

In addition to the echoes of the Israelites, an undercurrent of the Fall runs through this story. As with Eve ("Did God really say, 'You shall not eat from any of the trees in the garden'?"), Satan began by being reasonable: *Does God* Gn 3:1
really want you to starve in the desert? But where Eve listened and attempted to reason with the devil, Jesus called on the Gn 3:2–3
name of the Lord, quoting Scripture to defend himself. Just as Satan was logical and charming with Eve, Satan was clever with Jesus, twisting Scripture to serve his own needs. Jesus responded as Eve should have: *Get away, Satan!*

One verse in this passage resounds in the modern ear. "All these I shall give to you, if you will prostrate yourself and worship me." Many of us have been told that God will fulfill every longing of our heart if we are faithful; this verse sounds like just such a promise. The trouble is that it was spoken by Satan, not by the Lord. God does not promise to give us everything we want. When he says he will give us the desires of our hearts, it is contingent on one thing: Ps 37:4
that we delight ourselves in the Lord. If God is the desire of your heart, he will give you the desire of your heart. If we long for God, he will give himself to us. That is the promise. God and the Cross — that's what Christians are guaranteed. When we begin to insist that God give us everything we want, we have turned from the Gospel.

19. Preaching in Galilee: *Matthew 4:13–17*; Mark 1:14–15; Luke 4:14–15

News of what happened when Jesus was baptized had traveled fast as countless visitors returned home. They carried
tales of one whom John had called both Lamb of God and
Jn 1:29, 34 Son of God. They recounted wild stories of the heavens being torn open and God himself claiming this Nazarene as
Mt 3:16–17 his own. And so excitement began to build — was this what
John had meant when he had said, “The kingdom of heaven
Mt 3:2 is at hand”? Was this carpenter’s son coming to inaugurate a
new kingdom?

Talk like this couldn’t help but be repeated, in eager whispers or with loud denials. The Jews knew that they were living in the time of the Messiah, not just because they longed for him, but because the prophet Daniel had promised not only that the Messiah would come, but also when he would come.

The Book of Daniel tells the story of a wise young Jew
during the Babylonian Captivity. Soon after he was taken
into exile, Daniel became one of the advisers to King Ne-
buchadnezzar, who had a troubling dream that foretold the
Dn 2 end of his empire. Daniel explained the dream, in which
one empire replaced another until finally the fifth empire
triumphed, a kingdom not made by men that would nev-
Dn 2:44–45 er be destroyed. This empire was, of course, the Messianic
kingdom, the “kingdom of God,” or “kingdom of heaven”
in Matthew. The Jews had survived the rule of Babylon, Persia, and Greece. They were suffering now under Rome, the
fourth empire, but knew that the Messiah must come during
Roman rule.

Even better: Daniel had given a timeline. For seventy
weeks of years after the order that Jerusalem was to be re-
built, they would endure in affliction. But after those 490
Dn 9:24 years, “a holy of holies will be anointed” — the Messiah, an
Ex 28:41; anointed one in the vein of the priests and kings who had
1 Sm 10:1 been anointed in the glory days of Israel and Judah. This order was given around 457 BC, which means that at the time

of John the Baptist, around AD 30, the anticipation of those Jews who read Daniel in this way would have been near fever pitch — and compounded by the oppressive rule under which the Jewish people more than chafed. Seventy times seven years had passed, and the Jubilee of Jubilees was upon
them, when not only would slaves and land be redeemed, but Lv 25:10, 18
all Israel, indeed all the world.

The people knew that the Messiah would come to re-
store the Temple and defeat the enemies of God's people, Zec 6:12–13
a "prophet" like Moses through whom God would work Dt 18:15
an even greater exodus. He was to be a new Davidic *king*: 2 Sm 7:12–14; Ps
the Son of David and greater than David, the king whose 110:1; Is 11:1–10;
kingdom would last forever, a shepherd-king like David who Mt 22:41–46;
would gather the scattered children of Israel and draw even Am 9:11–12; Is
the Gentiles to the one true God. In this new Messianic 9:6; 35:1–10;
kingdom, the Messiah would bring not only peace and free- 61:1–3
dom but also miraculous healing, a world reborn. Though some Jews may have expected a warrior whose military and political savvy would free his people from the rule of Rome, most saw the Messiah as a spiritual figure as well as a temporal one, often expecting that the advent of the Messiah would effect a transformation in the world as a whole. They sought one who would be anointed as a new Aaronic *priest*, purifying Jewish worship and leading the people (and perhaps the world) back to God. These expectations continued to develop even after the Old Testament was written; the Essenes at Qumran were so driven by Messianic expectations that some texts indicate that they were looking for two simultaneous messiahs, one priestly and one kingly, at least one of whom was expected to "heal the wounded, and revive the dead, and bring good news to the poor."

So when John declared that this Messianic kingdom was at hand and placed it squarely on his cousin's shoulders, people were ready to listen. Then Jesus disappeared into the desert for forty days as the stories spread. Finally, he emerged from the desert, demanding that they repent.

Repent. It's the first word Jesus publicly proclaimed in Matthew's Gospel, and it's at the heart of his first statement in Mark as well, as he made it clear that he had come to free his people from sin even more than from suffering and oppression. But the people had listened to John's call of repentance without feeling judged, and they did the same with Jesus' call as he wandered through Galilee and spoke in their synagogues. They hung on his every word as he called them to believe in the *euangelion*, the good news not of Caesar's reign but of the kingdom of God, the kingdom prophesied by Daniel.

Jesus went first to Capernaum, which he would make his home base, because Capernaum lay in the north, in the land of Naphtali which had (with Zebulun) been the first to be
2 Kgs 15:29; Is 8:23 destroyed by the Assyrians. To the land that had been longest
Is 9:1 in darkness, Jesus first brought the light.

There's no talk yet of miracles, though the evangelists will begin telling us of them shortly. Up to this point Jesus had the people's attention not because of the wonders he worked but simply because of who he was and what he was saying. His message, like John's, was simple: Repent, for the kingdom of God is at hand. And though he called people to the hard work of conversion, they listened. They praised him. Before he worked a single miracle, something about him spoke to them, called to them. Perhaps it was his conviction, his compassion, his strength, his eloquence. There was something magnetic about this man, something far more beautiful than so much insipid art and storytelling has led us to believe. As the story continues to unfold, we'll begin to understand what it was about the Master that made so many follow.

20. Jesus Calls His First Disciples: John 1:35–51

From the beginning of his public ministry, people flocked to Jesus. Many of his followers are never named in Scripture, and we won't know their stories in this life, but a few of those first encounters were significant enough that the evangelists recounted them in detail. (There's some difficulty in determining the order of events here. Given the concrete connection the Synoptics make between Jesus' baptism and the temptation, I'm inclined to think that John's depiction of the testimony of John the Baptist to Jesus is a second event that took place after the temptation, as John the Baptist recounted what had happened when Jesus had been baptized.)

After he proclaimed Jesus to be Lamb of God and Son of God, John the Evangelist tells us of two followers of John Jn 1:29, 34
the Baptist who heard the Baptist testify to Jesus: Andrew the brother of Simon Peter and an unnamed disciple whom tradition holds to be John the Beloved. The Baptist and these two followers watched Jesus; again, the Baptist announced Jesus' role: "Behold, the Lamb of God." One imagines him Rv 5:12
looking at Andrew and John significantly and gesturing toward Jesus. Or maybe they didn't need his prompting. Maybe they were so drawn to Jesus that they took off after him without even taking their leave of John. Certainly, there was no debate, no request for further explanation. Something about John's simple assertion, "Behold, the Lamb of God," silenced their doubts and set them moving.

They didn't walk right up to Jesus. Instead, they followed him — awkwardly — at a distance, overwhelmed by the thought of approaching the Messiah. Perhaps there was a whispered argument over who ought to speak first or what they ought to say. But Jesus, taking pity on them, turned and spoke: "What are you looking for?"

These are his first words in John's Gospel, strikingly similar to his first words in Luke's. Jesus peered intently at Lk 2:49
these two men and asked them the question that is the beginning — and sometimes the end — of so many people's walks with him: "What are you looking for?" Are you seeking social status through church membership? You may find it, but it might not lead you to Jesus. Are you seeking quick solutions to the problems plaguing your out-of-control life? Again, Jesus might seem like the way out, but using him as a means to an end often means we make an idol of the living God and never encounter him as he truly is. When we're seeking popularity or stability or success, we're unlikely to

find it in Jesus; we're unlikely to find Jesus at all. But when we finally come to the point of seeking truth, seeking real love, seeking meaning, seeking mercy, then we'll end up following after him.

Andrew and John had no real answer to Jesus' question. They weren't quite sure what they were seeking. The Messiah, yes, but more than that. They were looking for God, and somehow this carpenter seemed to be the answer to the question they couldn't quite articulate but that haunted their lives just the same. But they couldn't exactly say that. So, with some degree of awkwardness, they answered his question with another question: "Where are you staying?" It wasn't the most dignified way to break the ice, but anything to talk to Jesus.

Clumsy though this response may have been, it was somehow just the right thing to say. Essentially, Jesus had asked them what they wanted, and they gave a pure and vulnerable and frightening answer: *We want you.* It wasn't eloquent or astute, but it was enough. Jesus invited them: "Come, and you will see." They would see far more than just the place he was sleeping that night. This God, who had
Jn 9:39 come "so that those who do not see might see," was promising that if they followed him, they would no longer walk in darkness.

Eagerly, Andrew went off to tell his brother, Simon Peter, about whom we will hear so much in chapters to come. "We have found the Messiah," he cried, the first to identify Jesus as the Christ in no uncertain terms. He brought
Jn 6:8–9 Peter to Jesus, as he later brought a little boy to Jesus, as
Jn 12:20–22 he brought some Greeks to Jesus. Andrew didn't need the spotlight; he was content to live in the shadows if it meant that every once in a while, he could bring someone to the Light.

The look that Jesus now gave to Peter must have been intense and penetrating. He saw Peter, and Peter knew that he was being seen — truly seen. Then, in a casual claim of divinity, Jesus gave Peter a new name. In the biblical tradition,

God is the one with the authority to change a person's name. Gn 17:5, 15;
Peter must have been startled, but John says nothing more in 32:29;
his account. Matthew had already written about Peter's new 2 Sm 12:24–25
name in his Gospel some years earlier; evidently, John thought Mt 16:16–20
Matthew's account was explanation enough.

Striking as the three men's encounter with Jesus was, this was not yet their call, their life-changing invitation to be disciples. They had been touched by Jesus but not yet asked to leave everything and follow. That would come soon enough. For now, they accompanied Jesus, free to come and go as they pleased; only later would they be made fishers of
men, leaving everything behind to follow him. Lk 5:10–11

In the meantime, Jesus continued to draw people to himself. In Galilee he found Philip, who had grown up in Bethsaida, the same small town as Peter and Andrew. There are no details here, no story of what drew Philip to Jesus or how Jesus convinced Philip of his identity. Jesus simply said, "Follow me," and Philip did. Such was the power of the Incarnate Word that Philip not only left his life behind, he also invited others to join him. Eagerly, he became an evangelist, inviting Nathanael to come and see "the one about whom Moses wrote in the law, and also the prophets."

There must have been some long and intense conversations behind the scenes for Philip to have been so convinced that Jesus was the one foretold by the holy men of old. But Nathanael was not so easily swayed. He was from Cana and evidently something of a snob. It didn't matter what Philip said, Nathanael simply could not believe that a hick from backwater Nazareth could be anyone worth talking about. Even this wild story about fulfilled prophecies and the Messiah walking among them couldn't sway him. After all, "Can anything good come from Nazareth?" But Philip was persistent, so, grudgingly, Nathanael went along.

This story may be one of the most startling in the Gospels: Nathanael wanted nothing at all to do with Jesus. Jesus said Nathanael had integrity and mentioned a fig tree. Suddenly, Nathanael was ready to pledge his life for this Nazarene.

We can't know exactly what happened here, but Nathanael's startled response to what might otherwise have just seemed a friendly overture gives the impression that Jesus' words were speaking to a particular wound in Nathanael's heart. Is it possible that Nathanael had been wrestling with just this question under the fig tree? If so, perhaps the scene played out like this:

Nathanael was convinced that his sins made him unworthy of the name "Israelite." He was dishonest and disloyal, to his friends and to his God. He stood one afternoon under a fig tree lamenting his faithless character when Philip interrupted him with some nonsense about a fool from Nazareth being the promised Messiah. Nathanael's disdainful response said more about his self-disgust than about his prejudices. But it was clear that Philip wasn't going to drop the issue, so Nathanael trudged along after him to see this alleged Messiah. They walked for some distance before they finally saw the man.

As he approached the young Nazarene, Nathanael's mind was clouded with his own troubles. His duplicity. His unworthiness to be called an Israelite.

"Here is a true Israelite. There is no duplicity in him."

The words cut through the fog of self-loathing that surrounded him. In a moment of absolute clarity, he locked eyes with the stranger. Surely it was just a coincidence. Nobody could know what he was struggling with. But this Jesus looked deep into his soul. He saw the wounds, the fear, and he called them out as lies.

Overwhelmed, Nathanael stammered, "How do you know me?"

"Before Philip called you, I saw you under the fig tree." *I saw you in your despair, and I have called you over to tell you: that is not who you are. You are a good man.*

If this (or something like this) is what happened, Nathanael's reaction begins to make sense. Not only could this

stranger read his mind, he could also see to the core wounds of Nathanael's heart and speak a healing balm over them. Jesus had given him peace through these words, and Nathanael knew that such peace was as miraculous as the Messianic liberty offered to captives and to the oppressed. Lk 4:18

"Rabbi, you are the Son of God; you are the King of Israel." This acclamation is remarkably similar to Peter's in Matthew 16. But where Peter was given the keys to the kingdom in Mt 16:16
response, Nathanael got only a promise: "You will see greater things than this." Only a promise — but what a promise!

Nathanael used the title "Son of God" as any Jew would: as a Messianic title. Kings of Israel were proclaimed on their
coronation days to be "sons of God" by adoption. Knowing Ps 2:7
nothing of Jesus' divinity, Nathanael was likely just proclaiming his belief that Jesus was the Davidic king to come. Even 2 Sm 7:14
this limited understanding was remarkable, as Nathanael proclaimed Jesus to be the anointed one sent by God to redeem Israel. But compared to Jesus' true divine identity, his Messiahship was nothing; Nathanael would see far greater things in his years of following Jesus. He would see Jesus, the Son of
Man, as the ladder between heaven and earth, the means by Gn 28:12
which God and man are united, the true fulfillment of the
long-ago dream of Jacob, himself the first Israelite and a man Gn 32:29
of great duplicity. Gn 27

Nathanael had heard the testimony of Philip, and maybe of the others as well. He'd heard about the voice that spoke from heaven when Jesus came out of the waters. But he did not believe until the Lord saw Nathanael's brokenness and still loved him. *Those things may be part of your story, but that is not who you are,* he heard. *You are loved.* There are millions in our world longing to hear the same thing, to have Jesus see their pain, love them in it, and — ultimately — love them out of it. As the Mystical Body of Christ, it's our job to speak this truth to the Nathanaels of the world and to let them hear Jesus speaking in us. First, though, we have to let Jesus do this for us.

Chapter Seven

JESUS THE WONDER-WORKER

21. The Wedding Feast at Cana: John 2:1–12

This next scene takes place "on the third day," a phrase that
relates it not only to the previous events but also points forward to the Resurrection. More subtly, there may be a reference to Exodus, where God revealed himself to the people on Ex 19:16–19
the third day, establishing a marriage covenant with them.
To this day, some Jewish communities commemorate this
event (on Shavuot, or the Feast of Weeks) with the reading
of a marriage certificate between God and his people, often
referencing some of the Old Testament passages that speak Hos 2:21–22;
of God as the bridegroom of his people Israel. Now Jesus the Is 54:5; 62:4–5
divine bridegroom comes to a wedding on the third day to Lk 5:34–35
begin his work of wooing and wedding his bride the Church. Rv 19:7, 21:9

The story starts rather simply with Jesus' mother being invited to a wedding in Cana. Jesus and his disciples were also invited, though they seem to have been rather an afterthought, an added dozen guests at the grand affair. A wedding in the ancient Near East was in some ways even more extravagant than the opulent affairs we see today. The celebration went on long into the night — and the next night and the next, usually between five and seven days. This kind of celebration would be costly, but the local understanding of hospitality made it shameful for a host not to provide lavishly for his guests. So when the wine began to run out, it was a catastrophe.

Mary's motherly heart ached for the family, especially for the young couple who would have to send their guests away early, their nuptials clouded with shame and a sense of failure. Fortunately, her son was there. Mary didn't tell Jesus what to do, didn't describe how he ought to produce the wine or specify what blend she was looking for. She simply pointed out the need, trusting that he would supply it as he saw fit.
"They have no wine," she said, a line that echoes the cry of
Is 24:11 Isaiah when he wrote of a world longing for the Messiah to
come and inaugurate the promised Messianic feast, filling
Is 25:6 his people with choice wine.

"Woman," Jesus called her, a title that surprises us but is
not one of disrespect. Jesus was speaking to Mary as the New
Gn 3:6 Eve, the woman whose yes reversed Eve's no in Eden. Before
Gn 2:23 the Fall, Eve was simply called "woman"; only after the Fall
Gn 3:20 do we hear her called Eve. Mary stands here as the unfallen
Woman, inviting the New Adam to begin undoing the damage wrought when the first woman invited the first Adam to sin. Still, Jesus is the one in control. "How does your concern affect me?" he responded. "My hour has not yet come."

Jesus seems uninterested in the couple's plight, until you
realize what he was saying. When Jesus spoke of his "hour,"
Mt 26:45; he meant the hour of his passion and death. "My hour has
Mk 14:35; not yet come" isn't a petulant refusal to bow to his mother's
Jn 7:30; 8:20; wishes; rather, it's a tender reassurance. *Mother, if I do this*
12:23; 13:1 *thing, it ends on Calvary. If I begin here, I will no longer be*
yours. I don't have to do this yet. Jesus knew that his first public miracle would set things into motion that would eventu-
Lk 2:35 ally pierce his mother's heart. He wanted to be sure that she
understood what she was asking. *Are you ready? Is this worth it?*

One might expect Mary to change her mind at this, deciding that people having more to drink wasn't worth the loss of her son. But she had borne him to offer him. In truth,

she'd been offering him back to the Father at least since she'd
brought him to the Temple to dedicate him to the Lord. Be- Lk 2:22
sides, the woman who would be made mother to us all on
Calvary already loved this bride and groom with a mother's Jn 19:26–27
love; she wanted to protect them. For love of his mother, Jesus was willing to delay; for love of her children, Mary asked him to go. And so Jesus took his first step on the road to the cross.

"Do whatever he tells you," Mary told the servants at the feast, her last recorded words and a fitting swan song. Those who love the Blessed Mother are gratified to see that one of her few interactions with the adult Jesus shows her to be an intercessor so powerful she managed to change God's plan (though, of course, he knew from all eternity what her intercession would accomplish that day). And yet the true message of Mary's life isn't one of asking and receiving, but one of following and obeying. To the people who had ratified their marriage covenant with the Lord on Sinai by saying, "We will do everything that the LORD. has told us" and Ex 24:3
failed in every generation, to every unfaithful Christian since Cana, to each one of us, she offers another chance. *Get up*, she says. *Try again.* "Do whatever he tells you."

Joseph's Pharaoh had said the same thing, telling the
Egyptians to do whatever Joseph told them. Joseph, who Gn 41:55
had been betrayed and sold by Judah; Joseph, who had stood Gn 37:26–28
condemned between two condemned men but had been ex- Gn 40
alted to the right hand of the king; Joseph, who ultimately Gn 41:43–44
saved his people and the world through grain that gave life. Gn 41:57
In the moments before Jesus provided for his people, we are reminded that he came as a new Joseph, to feed and strengthen and save his starving people as Joseph had.

Jesus turned to the servers and indicated some jars for ceremonial washing. "Fill the jars with water." They poured in water, gallon after gallon after gallon. But when they drew it out, it was the finest wine they had ever tasted. God is no miser when satisfying our needs. Jesus didn't make just enough wine to last the celebration. He made an appalling

amount — around 150 gallons, and of impeccable quality.
Here was the beginning of the Messianic feast, the wedding
feast of heaven where God supplies abundantly and revels in
Is 25:6–8; our joy. This wedding feast for all nations is no rejection of
Jl 4:18; the Old Covenant, though. John points out that the purpose
Am 9:13–14; of the jars was for ceremonial washing, an element of the
Rv 19:9 ritual purity-based Old Covenant. Jesus didn't break those
jars, disdaining what had gone before. He took the water of
the Old Covenant and transformed it into the wine of the
Lk 22:20 New Covenant. Though he was doing something new, it was
building on all that God had done before in preparing the
people of Israel to receive their God.

It's not the job of the wedding guests to provide their
own wine, though; the one who offers wine at a wedding
feast is the bridegroom. When Mary asked her son to give
wine to the guests, it wasn't merely a means of avoiding em-
barrassment for the couple or increasing the guests' enjoy-
ment. Mary was asking him to step forward as the bridegroom of Israel. Throughout the Old Testament, God had
revealed himself to Israel not merely as lawgiver but as lover,
Hos 2:21–22; as bridegroom of his people. When Jesus stood up at a wed-
Is 54:5; 62:4–5; ding feast and provided wine for the guests, he was begin-
Ez 16; Song of ning to show the world that he was the fulfillment of that
Songs image, the bridegroom of his people.

Rv 19:7, 21:9 Many of Jesus' miracles recounted in the Gospels are
enormous, life-changing affairs, but it's important that we
remember that his first public miracle was — relative to healing lepers and raising the dead — a comparatively small matter. There was no earth-shattering need here, just the frustration and discomfort of people he loved. God does not give
us everything we want; that's not the message of the Gospel.
But he's concerned with everything in our lives. He's aware
of our struggles, and though he might leave us in them, he
never leaves us there alone. And sometimes when we come to
him with a relatively trivial need, he supplies beyond all we
Eph 3:20 could ask or imagine.

This sign in Cana was a revelation of Jesus' glory, a

theophany on the third day as in Exodus and in the garden tomb. His disciples began to believe, a journey of deepening faith that would take years as they moved from accepting him as a sort of Messiah to worshipping him as Lord and God. But this first sign (with its clear nod to the first plague in Egypt) was the beginning of the new Exodus, by which Jesus, the new Moses, would lead his people out of slavery to sin and into the Promised Land of heaven. And it was the beginning of the revelation of Jesus the Bridegroom, the Lord and lover of souls.

Jn 20:28
Ex 7:20
Wis 11:26

22. Preaching and Healing in Capernaum: Matthew 8:14–17; *Mark 1:21–34*; Luke 4:31–41

Through all this, we've heard nothing more of Simon Peter, Andrew, James, or John. It seems that their interest in Jesus hadn't yet become a determined decision to give their lives over to him. But they had been marked, and it wouldn't be long before he called them not just to believe, but to follow.

Jesus had left his home of Nazareth and made his way to Capernaum, the town where Peter, Andrew, James, and John lived. Again, he taught in the synagogue, but his teaching was different from that of the scribes. The role of a good scribe was to recount what had already been said, either in Scripture or by others who interpreted it. Even the best of rabbis was respected for being able to quote many other learned men who had gone before. There was no dogma, no incontrovertible authority, and certainly no novelty. So when Jesus spoke, confidently and decisively, the people were astonished: This man spoke as though what he said really were true — as though because he said it, it was true.

Many of the people were impressed at Jesus' teaching; the demons were, too. There was a man in town who was possessed by a demon and began to cry out against Jesus. This demon had recognized something different about Jesus and realized that he was more than a teacher, he was "the Holy One of God." While this phrase had been used of Aaron the high priest and Elisha the prophet, the demon's

Ps 106:16;
2 Kgs 4:9

use of it indicates a sense that it was Jesus' true name. Indeed, it was only after the astonishing revelation of the Bread of Life discourse that the apostles were able to identify Jesus
Jn 6:69 this way. This title, then, seems to suggest something more than a priestly or prophetic vocation, something more akin to Jesus' true identity. Hoping to gain power over Jesus by using his true name, the demon cried out, "I know who you are — the Holy One of God!" But Jesus was far too powerful to be defeated by the demon's proclamation, and the evil one succeeded only in testifying to the identity of the Christ, proclaiming Jesus as the Messiah from the beginning of his public ministry.

Confronted with a demon, a Jewish exorcist would typically engage in long and complicated rituals with prayers, water, and burning herbs, beseeching God to set the possessed person free. Jesus simply spoke: "Quiet! Come out of him!" and the demon was cast out. Jesus needed no ritual, nor did he have to intercede with the Father. He had the power to defeat the demon himself.

Again, the people were *amazed* — a word used repeatedly to describe the reaction of the crowds to Jesus' teachings
Lk 5:9; Mk 10:24 and miracles. They had never seen someone command demons on his own authority. And word continued to spread: *This man is doing things that have never been done before.*

Jesus made his way through the excited crowd until he entered Simon Peter's house, where Simon's mother-in-law lay severely ill. Those who were worried about her interceded with him, and Jesus lifted her up to her feet. In Mark's account it was only then, only when she had trusted him enough to stand while terribly ill, that she was healed. Matthew and Luke show her rising in response to her healing, not lying there wonderstruck but moving immediately to wait on them. Either way, her response to the miraculous work of God in her life was service. May ours be the same.

It seems Jesus spent some quiet hours being served, as all three accounts point out that he went to Simon Peter's house after leaving the synagogue and that the crowds didn't

arrive until evening (when the Sabbath had ended and they
expected healing to begin). By then word had spread that
this wonder-worker was at the home of Simon the fisherman,
so people brought the sick and possessed to the door and
Jesus healed many, fulfilling several Old Testament prophecies that the Messiah would deliver God's people from their Ps 146:7-8;
afflictions. Matthew specifically connects this to Isaiah's Is 35:5–6; 42:6–7
fourth Servant Song, a text that (read in the light of the Pas- Is 53:4
sion) promises not just that Jesus would take away our suffering, but that he would do so by bearing our infirmities and
sufferings himself.

Jesus did not, it seems, cure them all. Apparently, he
knew that some would do better without being healed, at
that time or possibly ever. Though Jesus worked many miracles, both for love of the sick and to show his power, he is in
the business of saving souls, not merely bodies. Sometimes
he leaves us in our suffering in order to save our souls.

At the end of this night of healing, the evangelists tell us
that Jesus forbade the demons to speak so that they wouldn't
reveal that he was the Messiah. Here we have the first hint
of the Messianic Secret. Throughout his ministry, Jesus
spoke in riddles and allusions and parables to conceal his Mk 4:11–12;
identity from those who wouldn't understand. Many would Mt 27:11
be tempted to follow him because of the allure of political
power, but Jesus didn't want followers who were more con- Jn 6:14–15
cerned with the overthrow of Rome than with the overthrow
of sin. Others would seek to have him killed if they knew Jn 11:47–49
he was claiming to be God, and while he was ready to die
eventually, there was much to do and say before his hour
came. And there was the danger that if Rome got wind of a
man proclaiming himself to be the Messiah, Jesus' followers
might suffer along with him — a risk he was clearly willing Jn 11:16
to accept once they had been given a chance to hear and embrace the Good News, but not until then. So he gave hints
and left clues that would draw his disciples on and leave his
later followers poring over the Word until he comes again.
And for those who flocked to him in Capernaum, he spoke

not a word of revolution. Instead, he looked them in the eye, took them by the hand, listened to their grief, and spoke their names. And he healed them just as much by this ordinary acknowledgment of their dignity as he did by all the miracles he worked.

23. The Rejection at Nazareth: Matthew 13:54–58; Mark 6:1–6; *Luke 4:16–30*; John 4:43–44

Everywhere he went, Jesus was greeted with enthusiasm. People flocked to the synagogue to hear him preach, hopeful that this, at last, was the Messiah, the one who would end their exile and set them free from all oppression. News was traveling fast of the Messianic figure speaking of the kingdom of God, and many of those who heard of it were eager to see him for themselves, to find out what they needed to do and how they could help him bring this revolution about.

But in his hometown, people were less enthusiastic. They remembered his ordinary childhood. Perhaps they had always thought him wise, but this was no Messiah. This was the carpenter, old Joseph's boy. Let the other towns in Galilee say what they like, Nazareth was unconvinced.

As he had in every town, as he likely had every Sabbath
of his adult life, Jesus went to the synagogue. It was custom-
ary for different men to read from the word of God, and
Jesus did just that. He asked for a scroll of Isaiah and found
Is 61:1–2; 42:7 two passages that he read in quick succession.

It was a reading about the Messiah, anointed by the
Spirit of God. To the people who had heard about God's
Lk 3:22 Spirit resting on Jesus at his baptism, the allusion was unmis-
takable. And now this alleged Messiah, speaking in the first
person, announced that he had come to preach the Gospel,
Is 61:1 the *euangelion*, to the poor. He would liberate captives (and,
they hoped, those in exile). He would give sight to the blind,
Is 42:7; 61:1–2 set the oppressed free, and proclaim a jubilee year, a year
when debts were released, slaves set free, and ancestral land
Lv 25 returned.

Then Jesus sat, in the posture of an authoritative teacher,

and gave the world's shortest and most incendiary homily: "Today this scripture passage is fulfilled in your hearing."

Jesus looked at the women who had changed his diapers and the men who had played peekaboo with him and confidently told them that he was the Messiah, the one who would set Israel free. These people thought of him as that sweet kid down the block and remembered what his toddler lisp sounded like. Many could recall the minor scandal that had arisen when Mary and Joseph had gotten married so quickly and then disappeared for a few years.

It's always hard to change our perspective on someone we think we know, but they did. They heard him speak with power, and they listened. Yet even as they spoke so highly of him, they couldn't shake their memories of him. *Where did he learn all this? How does he work all the miracles we've heard about? Don't we know his mother? And his other relatives? Is that really Joseph's boy?* To this last, of course, the answer was "not exactly."

But their approval seems to have been rather self-interested. Jesus knew this, of course, and rather than basking in their praise, he immediately pointed out their true motive. *Yes, you all believe in me, don't you?* he seems to be saying. *Might it have something to do with the miracles you've been hearing about? You know, Elijah and Elisha didn't spend their time working miracles in their hometowns.*

It's deliberately provocative, the first time we have a sense that Jesus was far more concerned with *why* people followed him than *that* they followed him. As we'll see again and again, he'd much rather have a small band of true disciples than thousands of fickle hangers-on. Jn 6:66–67

Jesus didn't actually refuse to do any miracles in Nazareth; he just implied that he would refuse, mentioning how the prophets of old often served pagans rather than their own neighbors. But his neighbors knew just what he meant: For all his words about healing and liberation, he was offering them nothing. Thirty years they had worked alongside him, joked with him, listened to him opine, and were they to get nothing out of it? They were furious. Like most of us, they wanted Jesus not for who he was but for what he could do for them. And when he refused to perform on command, they wanted nothing to do with him.

On top of that, he'd implied that he would do for pa-
Is 61:2 gans what he wouldn't do for them. In quoting Isaiah, he'd skipped the part about God's vengeance and had followed it with talk of healing the Gentiles. To their minds, that made him a traitor.

It's the first moment of heartbreak that we see in the adult life of Jesus. These people whom he loved so desperately wanted only to use him. When he wouldn't be used, they were angry enough to kill. It was a harbinger of what was to come, both on Calvary and in the hearts of believers the world over. Sometimes, perhaps God says no to our earnest prayers so that we may choose to love him for who he is and not merely for what he does.

Jesus had little time to spare for sorrowful nostalgia here. The people he had loved his whole life were forming a mob to throw him off a cliff, all because he hadn't become their genie. He let them drive him out of town and up the hill, giving them time to repent of the blows they were raining down on him. But their minds were made up; they would not turn back from their murderous intent. Still, it wasn't yet his time. So in a supernatural act that somehow never gets credit as a miracle, Jesus walked away from a murderous mob. He walked right through their midst, and not one of them could raise a hand to stop him. Though the ones he loved tried to kill him, he didn't end up dead. It wasn't, of course, the only time that such a thing would happen.

Maybe he made them feel some shame. Maybe a few even repented. Mark tells us that he didn't work many miracles there, only healing a few sick people. It's possible that he had done that before his appearance in the synagogue, but surely somebody would have pointed that out to the mob.

No, it must have been after his brush with death. It

seems Jesus was walking away from his childhood friends,
dejected over their lack of faith, when he saw a few stragglers,
sick people who couldn't make it up the hill or who hadn't
wanted to hurt him. Jesus had every right to shake the dust
of Nazareth from his feet, but he looked with love on those Mt 10:14
few who truly suffered, and he gave them what they needed
— not merely a healing, but a quiet moment alone with the
Savior. Nazareth was not lost yet, and those few he healed
would have work to do to soften the hearts of their angry
neighbors. As for Jesus, he had other places to preach, other
people to heal. And from this point on, he truly had no place
to lay his head. He had become a pilgrim like us, and now Lk 9:58
that his own people refused to accept him, he was united Jn 1:11
with us in the wandering that plagues us all, strangers and Heb 11:13–16;
sojourners that we are in this world. The one who hung the Eph 2:19;
stars in the sky became a homeless man. For us. To enter into Gn 23:4
our brokenness and show us the way home.

Chapter Eight

Jesus Makes Himself Known

24. The Call of Peter: Matthew 4:18–22; Mark 1:16–20; *Luke 5:1–11*

At this point, Simon Peter and his friends had seen some remarkable things: casting out of demons, powerful preaching,
healing, even a miracle that hit close to home. Still, every Lk 4:31–41
evening they headed to their boats to go about their business.
Jesus was a fascinating character and this was an exciting
time, but they needed to go on with their lives.

One morning, after a long and fruitless night of fishing, the men were washing their nets. They had caught nothing and discouragement may have been threatening to overwhelm them when up walked their new friend. He had been preaching and the crowd was too large to hear him well — would Peter row him out a ways so Jesus could have some space to breathe and his voice could be amplified by the water to reach more of the crowd?

Surely the man who walked away from a raging mob Jn 8:59; Lk
could have convinced the crowds to back up. And the one 4:29–30
who would calm the storm could have no difficulty raising Mk 4:35–41
his voice. But in this moment, he chose to need Peter. As the
exhausted Peter slumped in his boat, Jesus taught. When it
was finally over, Peter must have been eager to get home and

to bed, but Jesus had another idea. "Put out into deep water," he said, "and lower your nets for a catch."

This was too much. Peter was happy to listen to the young preacher speak about forgiveness and justice and even purity, but the man was a carpenter! He didn't know the first thing about fish. Sure, he could do some impressive things with sick people, but fishing was Peter's domain.

And yet. He had cured Peter's mother-in-law. Peter owed it to the man at least to humor him. Still, he had to voice his doubt for the plan. *Master, we haven't caught anything all night. But if you insist …*

With a sigh, Peter threw his net back out, knowing that the fish in the Sea of Galilee fed at night and would be impossible to catch at this time of the morning. To his great shock, the nets snagged on something. On many somethings. On fish beyond imagining, so many fish that their well-maintained nets were beginning to tear. So many fish that he and Andrew couldn't drag the nets in on their own. They called out to their partners, James and John, hollering for the two men to come help. Even with a second boat, there were so many fish that Peter worried their boats would sink. It was the greatest catch any among them had ever seen.

That was enough for him. Peter didn't know much about demons or palsies or fevers, but he knew fish. He knew that what he had just witnessed was impossible. Any man who wielded that type of power over creation was far more than just a man.

We would expect him to have run up to Jesus and begged to be saved. He ought to have offered his life in service to the King. But Peter is the most human of characters, and the evangelists don't shy away from showing us his flaws, perhaps to reassure us that God can use even the most broken vessels.

Peter fell down before Jesus and begged him: *Go away.*

Instead of "Master" he now called Jesus "Lord," a word used to show great deference to men and to refer to God himself. But Peter's new awareness of Jesus' power didn't im-

mediately draw him to give his heart to the Lord. Instead, he
was terrified. "Depart from me, Lord, for I am a sinful man,"
he said, experiencing a profound moment of self-knowledge
that echoes Isaiah's when he encountered God in his glory. Is 6:3–5

Peter was suddenly aware of his sin, aware that he had
no business in the presence of one as holy and powerful as Jesus. More than this, he seemed convinced that whatever Jesus
was about to ask of him, he would be a failure. It's one of the
few moments of humility that we see in Peter before the story
of Jesus reaches its climax. Peter was a brash fisherman who
would later try to talk Jesus out of dying. He would look Jesus Mt 16:22
in the eye at the Last Supper and insist that he didn't need
prayer. Like the Good Shepherd, he said, he would lay down Jn 10:15
his life for the Lord; within six hours, he was denying Jesus so Jn 13:37
emphatically that he perjured himself to save his skin. But here Mk 14:71
he left behind the grasping and the posturing and said, in all
humility, *I don't think I can be who you need me to be.*

Fortunately for Peter and for all of us, God doesn't seek
perfect followers but followers who are willing to repent,
willing to let him supply the grace. "Do not be afraid," Jesus 2 Cor 12:9
said, "from now on you will be catching men." *Don't worry,
Peter. I have something enormous to ask of you, but I will make
it possible. Just follow.*

Andrew was right there on the boat with them, quietly
watching this scene unfold. A few feet away were James and
John, Peter's partners who were only there because Peter had
recognized his weakness and asked them for help. This is
the pattern of Christian community that's set out for us at
the beginning. The Baptist sent Andrew to Jesus. Andrew
invited Peter. Peter needed James's and John's help. They Jn 1:35–42
were all interconnected, all weak at points and strong at others, sometimes leading and sometimes following. It's likely that Jesus would have called James and John even if they hadn't been there that day, but it's just possible that Peter's willingness to acknowledge his need for help is what drew Saint John to Jesus and gave us John's beautiful Gospel, his epistles, and the Book of Revelation. Our weakness is a gift,

not just to us but to those who will be called to serve us.

This miraculous catch was a watershed moment in the lives of these fishermen. "Come after me," Jesus said, "and I will make you fishers of men." Immediately, they followed.
Mk 1:20 They left their nets and their boats and their father behind and, thinking nothing of their past or their future, fixed their eyes on Jesus. For the time being, at least, they had no second thoughts. This Jesus they'd watched at some distance had called them, and suddenly they understood: He was worth everything. They left family and livelihood and hopes for the future behind. Because there was something about Jesus. For the new disciples, Jesus could no longer be an interesting teacher they kept tabs on. God could no longer be a distant force who held the stars in the sky. God had come into their lives, looked them in the eye, and asked them to follow. They couldn't stay on the fence any longer. They had to choose one way or the other.

In the rabbinic tradition, rabbis didn't go out looking
Jn 1:43; Mt 9:9 for disciples as Jesus did here and elsewhere. They, like their Greek and Roman contemporaries, waited for young men to approach them seeking wisdom. But Jesus came to seek and
Lk 19:10 save all the lost, not just the ones who knew they were lost. He didn't only want scholars and philosophers, he wanted fishermen and tax collectors. He wanted Pharisees and Zealots. He wanted everyone. So he broke with tradition (as he
Acts 4:13 so often would) and called uneducated, ordinary men like these, men who didn't know how much they needed him.

As we'll see throughout the Gospels, Jesus is in the busi-
Lk 1:52 ness of exalting the humble and lifting up the lowly — a fact that can seem rather unfair until we realize that we are all lowly, and that when our pride is cast down it's more of a gift than a curse (though it may take us some time to realize it). In calling these four, Jesus wasn't just setting up ordinary fishermen as the leaders of his new kingdom, but fishermen from Galilee, out of which (the chief priests and Pharisees
Jn 7:52 insisted) "no prophet arises." In God's economy, no hometown disqualifies you from holiness, no nationality or race

or disability or checkered past. But "God chose the lowly and despised of the world, those who count for nothing, to reduce to nothing those who are something." Whatever you think disqualifies you, it's a lie. God has called you, too — on purpose, just as you are.

1 Cor 1:28

25. Jesus Leaves Capernaum: *Mark 1:35–39*; Luke 4:42–44

Throughout his public ministry, we see Jesus going off to pray alone. Luke even points out that it's something he regularly did. He had deep need of communion with the Father and of withdrawing from the world in order to find God in prayer. How much more do we, who are not God, need to make time for silence and stillness to center ourselves in the Lord.

Lk 6:12; Mt 14:13, 23 Lk 5:16

At this point in Mark's Gospel, Jesus was preparing to leave Capernaum, where he seems to have had some degree of stability. So he got up before dawn and went to a deserted place to pray. But Simon Peter and the others weren't far behind him. Indeed, Mark says they "pursued" him. These same men who were previously content to spend most of their time going about their own business were now hungry to spend time with the Lord. As is often the case for those engaged in active ministry (which might be priesthood or motherhood, or a job as a teacher or nurse or maintenance worker or accountant), his prayer was interrupted by people who needed him. The disciples wanted to be with him, but they were also relaying the message that others were looking for him.

Wis 16:28

One can imagine Jesus taking a deep breath before heading back into the fray. The one who had spent thirty years with the freedom to be still, who had spent eternity communing with the Father and the Holy Spirit, would no longer have the privilege of the long hours of silence for which his human soul longed. But he gathered himself and set off, leaving Capernaum for the towns of Galilee and Judea, where so many longed to see him (little though they may have known it). For this he had come, not just to die and rise, but to proclaim the kingdom, to dwell with us, to teach and heal and love us in the flesh.

The people of Capernaum tried to stop him, both because of the miracles he worked and because of the peace that his presence brought to their weary souls. It may have been a joy to be wanted, especially after his terrible reception
Lk 4:16–30 in Nazareth. Or perhaps Jesus was drained and overwhelmed by the grasping crowds. But whether or not he wanted — at some level — to stay and be only theirs, he had to be about
Lk 2:49 his Father's business. His work was far more than just healing a handful of people in a small town in Galilee. He had to keep moving, keep preaching the good news of the king-
Lk 1:79; dom of God, that Messianic kingdom that would bring both
Mt 10:34 peace and the sword.

26. The First Cleansing of the Temple: John 2:13–25

Jesus' work of preaching took him all over the land of Israel. In John's Gospel, we're told of four visits he made to
Jn 2:13; 5:1; Jerusalem, though the Synoptics don't mention any ministry
10:22; 12:12 in Jerusalem until Holy Week. But John's Gospel tells of a number of Jewish festivals for which Jesus traveled to the holy city, and so Jerusalem features more strongly. The first time we see the adult Jesus in Jerusalem is for the Passover feast, the holiday that commemorated Israel's liberation from slavery in Egypt and her protection from death by means of
Ex 12:1–16; the blood of the unblemished lamb of God slaughtered to
1 Pt 1:18–19 save his people. This holy day figures strongly in all of the Gospels, but John in particular shows us the powerful work Jesus did in connection with the feast that he would eter-
Jn 6:4 nally transform by his passion. Jesus had been to Jerusalem
Lk 2:41 at Passover many times, but all those had been before his baptism, before Cana, before his public ministry had begun. This time, he was a public figure. This time, he was there not just to worship, but to teach.

On some level, he must have been used to the circus that had been made out of the Temple area. In the Court of the

Gentiles (the outer part of the Temple where God-fearing Gentiles were permitted to worship), there was a crowd of stalls. There were money-changers who took the people's Roman coins and exchanged them for the silver coins required at the Temple — for a fee. There was livestock, making livestock noises and livestock waste while their vendors made a pretty penny off those who couldn't bring their own sheep or doves with them from the country, or whose offerings were found wanting. It was not unusual for the people to be cheated of their money and of the peace that this holy place ought to have offered them. We might have some sense of the scene if we imagined snake oil salesmen haranguing parishioners as they made their way to their pews, trying to sell them livestock within the nave of the church and doing it all in the name of God.

Jesus' reaction was similar to what ours might be. This desecration had to stop. He drove them out. The sheep, the oxen, the men, all of them. He knocked over their coffers and made a scourge out of cords to show them how serious he was. "Stop making my Father's house a marketplace," he demanded. Animals needed to be sold, yes, and money to be changed; the law required silver coins of a purity found only (at the time) in the Tyrian shekel. But none of it had to be done in this sacred space. And none of it had to be done at
the expense of making space for all peoples to pray in God's Is 56:7
house.

It shouldn't have been possible for a lone man to drive out every one of the merchants. They should have banded together, fought back. But there was something about Jesus in this moment that made defiance impossible — something about the righteous anger flashing in his eyes or the power that seemed to radiate from him. The vendors shrank away as they listened to him, then snatched up what wares they could and made for the exits, in fulfillment of the prophecy of Zechariah that on the day of the Lord "no longer will
there be merchants in the house of the LORD of hosts." Such Zec 14:21
an absence was so remarkable, it merited its place as the last

word in Zechariah's book, but Jesus accomplished it with an angry glare and a whip made of cords. We who view Jesus merely as a sweet snuggler of lambs would do well to remember that he is fierce as well as tender.

Interestingly, none of the Temple officials seemed to ob-
Mk 11:15–19 ject very strenuously. At Jesus' return the week before his
death to cleanse the Temple again, his opponents would re-
Mk 11:18 solve to murder him. But here in the first year of his minis-
Lk 11:37–54; try, there was still an openness. He hadn't yet condemned the
Mk 3:1–6; 7:18–19 leading figures in the land, hadn't yet questioned their tradi-
Mk 11:18 tions or threatened the status quo. The priests and scribes
were intrigued rather than enraged, asking, "What sign can
you show us for doing this?" They, too, were awaiting a Messiah, though some of the most powerful among them weren't
terribly eager for an outsider to change things up, whatever
good it might bring for the nation as a whole.

Besides, the Jewish people were exceedingly familiar
with the concept of prophets proclaiming uncomfortable
Is 20; Jer 13; Ez 4 truths and performing odd deeds to go along with them.
They were open to the idea that Jesus was a reformer inspired
by God, but they wanted some evidence, something beyond
Mt 3:16–17 the reputation that his dramatic baptism had won for him.
Some of them may have been at the Jordan that day; the others would have heard tell of it. But an odd noise from heaven
wasn't anointing enough for them — they wanted proof.

Though Jesus worked many miracles, he never did them
just to prove a point. So when the Jews asked for a sign, his
response was more enigmatic than theatrical: "Destroy this
temple and in three days I will raise it up." At the very moment when he was taking possession of his Father's house,
when he was putting a temporary stop to the sacrificial worship there as a sign of its coming to an end with his sacrifice
on the cross, Jesus was promising his resurrection — he who
Mt 12:6 was greater than the Temple. His passion, death, and resurrection would prove his authority far better than any of his
other miracles.

At this point, nobody was enraged, though later they

would distort this prophecy and use it to execute first Jesus and later Saint Stephen the Protomartyr. Mt 26:59–61; Acts 6:14 But there was nothing sacred about the position of the vendors' stalls, and though Jesus had made space for the Gentiles to worship in the court allotted to them, he hadn't said anything to that effect; that would wait until his return to cleanse the Temple a second time, when he would quote Isaiah's prophecy that God's house would be "a house of prayer for all peoples." Is 56:7; Mt 21:13 Even his phrase "my Father's house" could be overlooked. Indeed, the same actions that caused people to plot his death later in his ministry here led people to believe in him. Jesus remained on his guard, though, knowing that many of these people were far more concerned with miracles than with conversion. As the creator of human nature and the possessor of a human nature, he was wise to the inclinations of the human heart. He wanted followers who were ready to hand their lives over in love, not people looking for a good show.

Jesus walked away from a much-disturbed Temple, knowing that what he had done wouldn't affect the way of things for more than a few days. But his outburst had been a call to action. He had come to his Father's house and found it unclean. Like the Levitical priests when a house had mold or mildew (a "fungal infection"), he ordered the house to Lv 14:33–36 be cleared out. He was giving the people a chance to make things right, to live with their hearts fixed on God and to allow the Gentiles to worship. Like the priests, he would be back to see what had become of the house. Lv 14:39

27. The Encounter with Nicodemus: John 2:23—3:21

Having left the Temple area, Jesus continued his work. His teaching had been catching people's attention, but Pharisees weren't in the habit of getting doctrinal insights from the latest alleged Messiah. So when Nicodemus's heart stirred within him at Jesus' words, he made arrangements to meet the Lord at night. Maybe it was cowardice, maybe prudence. Whatever the cause of Nicodemus's hesitation, it was overcome by his desire to speak with Jesus.

As so often happens in reading the Gospel accounts, we have to wonder: What sort of man must Jesus have been? How did he speak, how did he look at Nicodemus that caused this Pharisee, this leader among the Jews, this grounded, responsible, prudent man to come wandering in the darkness, longing to know more about the man the others disdained? It's probably a good thing we don't know the answers to these questions. It saves us from trying to make ourselves in the image of Jesus' personality traits while failing to imitate his love and meekness. And it certainly keeps us coming back, poring over the Scriptures to try to know him better. God is a mystery in the way one's spouse is a mystery: not impenetrable, but inviting.

For Nicodemus, this mystery was full of the theoretical. He came to Jesus with a profession of faith: "We know that you are a teacher who has come from God." But Jesus wanted to push him, so he launched into a dialogue that left Nicodemus puzzled and the rest of the world entranced.

"No one can see the kingdom of God without being born from above," Jesus said, though the Greek might also be translated "born again." This is just what Nicodemus thought, and his overly literal understanding made for an awkward image. But Jesus explained again. "No one can enter the kingdom of God without being born of water and Spirit." Jesus was telling this Pharisee that life with God was more than a matter of Jewish birth. One who seeks God's kingdom has to be born again through baptism.

Nicodemus remained perplexed, and Jesus pointed out the weakness of the human mind in the face of the things of God. Even the educated, the teachers of Israel, couldn't understand. "If I tell you about earthly things and you do not believe, how will you believe if I tell you about heavenly things?"

There's a certain harshness here, a rebuke of those who claim to be knowledgeable while failing to understand so much. Nicodemus was a bit ahead of his peers, but even he had only enough faith to sneak through the darkness to make his profession of faith. It wasn't much in the way of creeds, just a belief that Jesus was from God — that is, that he wasn't crazy or a charlatan.

Still, Jesus gave him a tremendous gift: a prophecy found only here in all the New Testament, entrusted to Nicodemus alone. "Just as Moses lifted up the serpent in the desert, so must the Son of Man be lifted up, so that everyone who believes in him may have eternal life."

To the man who had made knowledge of the books of Moses his life's work, Jesus offered a revelation, shedding light on a strange incident. While wandering in the desert, the Israelites had complained against God and their sin had reaped its reward: Venomous serpents entered the camp and began to attack. As a remedy for the bites, the Lord prescribed an inscrutable ritual: "Make a seraph and mount it on a pole, and everyone who has been bitten will look at it and recover." Nm 21:4–9

Rabbis at the time of Jesus remained unsure about the meaning of this bronze serpent, but they came to the conclusion that in looking upon the serpent, the Israelites were raising their eyes to heaven; the Book of Wisdom describes it as "a sign of salvation" through which God saved his people. Wis 16:5–8 Later Jewish thinkers explained that the episode demonstrates that God's power is so great he can even use the cause of a sickness to heal it.

According to Jesus, they were more right than they realized. When the Israelites looked at the bronze serpent, they were lifting their eyes to God and being healed by the same thing that brought their affliction. When Jesus was lifted up on the cross, the sign of salvation, the world would look upon God himself, and by means of our sin we would be saved from our sins.

Even more, the Torah makes it clear that by rebelling against God, the Israelites deserved what they got. Though the ancient Israelites expressed all things in active terms, implying that God deliberately willed all that came to pass, we might understand "the Lord sent snakes" to mean "the Lord stopped holding back the snakes." Those who've spent much time in the desert know that venomous creatures abound there. God had been protecting his people, but when they complained against him, he gave them a glimpse of what their time in the desert would have looked like without his protection. In instructing his people to look upon the bronze serpent, he was essentially saying, *Look to heaven and remember from what my mercy has saved you.* When he was crucified, Jesus would invite all people to fix their eyes on him and realize that he had died the death they deserved. This realization leads to repentance and newness of life.

John now moves us out of the conversation with Nicodemus into his own theological reflections. We don't know how Nicodemus responded to Jesus' explanation of the bronze serpent, nor whether he was willing that night to commit to more than "you are a teacher who has come from God." We don't know if he nodded pensively, shook his head in disgust, or thrilled at this revelation. After this scene, Nicodemus disappears from the story for several chapters. The next time we hear from him, he'll be speaking in defense of Jesus (though
Jn 7:50–51 with little risk to his own standing) — a follower of Jesus, perhaps, but still in secret, following under cover of darkness. Ultimately, though, Nicodemus made his choice. After Jesus'
Jn 19:39–40 death, Nicodemus declared himself a disciple and (according to tradition) was eventually martyred and honored as a saint. Some conversions take longer than others. But though Jesus knew well that his evening with Nicodemus would take years to bear fruit, he was in no rush to move on. Even if Nicodemus had never come to faith, that evening would have been worth the effort. Because love is never a waste of time.

Nicodemus's fledgling faith leads John into what may be the most iconic Bible verse: "For God so loved the world that he gave his only Son, so that everyone who believes in him might not perish but might have eternal life." For John, as for all the Evangelists, it's clear that God's motive in all things is love. Jesus was sent into the world not to deride it for its sin and be done; rather, he came to save it, to offer the gift of the Father's love and mercy to every human soul without exception.

Still, sin is sin. And those who attempt to speak God's love without calling people to repentance will find themselves preachers of a very different Gospel indeed. John's mention of the desperate love of God, love so strong it sent its only-begotten Son as a sacrifice, is closely tied to this truth: Receiving that love means accepting Jesus and living as he commands. This is how we come into the light — not just by believing that Jesus is God but by giving him our lives. May we, like Nicodemus, move out of the darkness and into the light.

Chapter Nine

Jesus the Teacher

28. The Sermon on the Mount — The Beatitudes: *Matthew 4:23—7:29*; Mark 3:7–12; Luke 6:17–26

Jesus continued his itinerant ministry, traveling particularly through Galilee as he taught and preached and healed. His fame spread throughout Galilee and Judea but also into Gentile country. Gentiles, too, journeyed to see him, bringing their sick and demon-possessed. It was as though the whole world was being drawn to Jesus.

And now that he had their attention, it was time to begin calling them to holiness. What does it look like to be a disciple? How do followers of Jesus forgive? How do they pray? How do they serve? These teachings are collected above all in the Sermon on the Mount, variously described in Luke as a sermon on the plain and in Mark as a sermon by the sea. There is no difficulty here: A traveling preacher will always repeat himself, so all three of these events could have taken place. Lk 6:20–49; Mk 4:1–34

For Matthew, the setting on the mountain is significant. Just as Moses had gone up Mount Sinai to receive the law, the new Moses is here sharing the law of the New Covenant. But he's also preparing his followers for a revolution. Revolutionaries at the time of Jesus took to the mountains to gather Ex 19:20; 24:12–18 followers and give speeches rousing them to action. With all he'd been saying and doing and all the Old Testament types he'd been fulfilling, the followers of Jesus were already expecting a revolution. When he took them to the mountains to teach them, they must have been ready for marching orders; they certainly weren't anticipating a revolution of mercy and purity and goodness.

Yet that's exactly what they got. Jesus began his most pivotal sermon with the Beatitudes, eight words of blessing that couldn't have been terribly reassuring to those followers of his who were eager to take up the sword. There were no accolades given to the fierce or the brave, only promises
made to the poor and the meek. Jesus, who had gathered a
Mk 1:15 following by promising the coming of God's kingdom, now
sat his followers down and clarified: This was not going to look like what they expected. There would be no swords, no bravado. The mighty would reap no spoils. Instead, he told his followers to fix their hearts on mercy, peace, and righteousness.

It's easy to imagine Jesus looking around at a group of people who were satisfied with themselves in one way or another, making deliberate eye contact with each one. To those who felt secure in their riches, he said, "Blessed are the poor
in spirit." Perhaps they didn't need to give everything away
Lk 18:22 (though it wouldn't be the only time he asked such a thing),
but they needed to be detached from their riches, to be openhanded in the recognition that even in their wealth they were completely dependent on God. Those who struggled in their poverty, on the other hand, were encouraged to let go of fear and bitterness, to be poor in spirit and not just materially poor.

To those who mourned and to those who refused to love deeply for fear of being hurt, Jesus offered consolation. To them all, Jesus said, "Blessed are they who mourn." The pain of losing a loved one can be agonizing, but the consolation
brought by the love of God is a balm to that wound. Those
Prv 4:23 who guard their hearts by refusing to love also never find the

healing God's love brings to the broken heart.

To revolutionaries ready to fight for their land, Jesus spoke very directly, echoing the psalm that ought already to Ps 37:11 have convicted them: "Blessed are the meek, / for they will inherit the land." Meekness is not weakness, not timidity or cowed compliance. Meekness is strength under control, power put under authority. Moses is described as being "very Mt 11:28–29 humble, more than anyone else on earth," despite his incli- Nm 12:3 nation at times to yell and break tablets. But he had sub- Ex 32:19 mitted the power of his fiery (and occasionally murderous) Ex 2:12 personality to the Lord and thus brought his people to their land. Zealots and other revolutionaries at the time of Christ thought the only way to regain possession of the Promised Land was to slaughter their oppressors. Jesus told them here: There is another way.

To those who were pleased with themselves because of their good reputations, Jesus offered a challenge not to be content with mere propriety but to long for holiness: "Blessed are they who hunger and thirst for righteousness." Your reasonably good life will only leave you unsatisfied, but if you strive for virtue, you will be filled.

To the righteous who had been wronged and had responded with vengeance, Jesus said, "Blessed are the merciful, / for they will be shown mercy." You may act as though you've done nothing that needs forgiving, but the Lord sees into your heart. If you refuse to show mercy to your neighbor, neither will mercy be shown to you. Perhaps in that crowd there were also those who had shown mercy but wondered if it had really been weakness, if they ought to have sought revenge instead. To these also Jesus spoke, though to them it might have felt more reassuring than convicting.

To all whose behavior was blameless but whose hearts were mired in lust, whose prayer and sacrifice were tainted by impure thoughts, he promised a better way: "Blessed are the clean of heart, / for they will see God." All their prayer, all their study of the Torah, all their visits to Jerusalem seemed empty, despite their ritual cleanliness. But if they offered the

Lord their hearts, if they sought not just physical but spiritual purity, they would finally see God, in this life and in the next. As with much of Jesus' teaching, this wasn't revolutionary; in the Old Testament, too, God had called his people to
Ps 24:4-5; 73:1 have not merely pure hands but pure hearts. Here, Jesus was reminding them of what they ought to have known already.

To any who enjoyed drumming up trouble between their neighbors, who delighted in the drama and gossip that resulted, Jesus said, "Blessed are the peacemakers." They may not be the first to know everything that happens in town, and they may not have the disordered pleasure of manipulating their neighbors, but they will be called children of God. Such language seems ordinary to us, but the phrase "children
Ps 29:1; 82:6 of God" is remarkably rare in the Old Testament in refer-
2 Sm 7:14; Ps 2:7 ence to human beings who weren't kings. This was a radical, world-changing promise.

To the people afraid of what their family would say when their allegiance to Jesus was discovered, he said, "Blessed are they who are persecuted for the sake of righteousness." To us who may not suffer because of our religious affiliation but suffer because of the ways we've chosen to be faithful, he says the same. Like being poor in spirit, fighting for what is just leads you to the kingdom of heaven, to the Promised Land.

Matthew's Gospel shows Jesus addressing only his disciples at the beginning of the Sermon on the Mount, but by the end he "dismissed the crowds." There may have been dozens or hundreds of people, each with his own story, each with his own internalized lies. These eight Beatitudes have served as a call to holiness for billions of Christians across the world over two millennia. They speak truth to the darkest places in our hearts. They call us out of the patterns of power the world has set out for us and into lives patterned after Christ's life. Above all, they invite us into the heart of the Father. Jesus referenced the Father seventeen times in the Sermon on the Mount, each time speaking to us as his brothers and sisters as he taught us how to live as children of the Father. There is no better way to do that than to seek to become men and women of the Beatitudes.

At the end of the Beatitudes, Jesus shifted from third person to second, speaking not of those who might consider themselves peacemakers or pure of heart but to every single person there: "Blessed are you when they insult you and persecute you and utter every kind of evil against you [falsely] because of me. Rejoice and be glad, for your reward will be great in heaven." Try though you might, you may never be given the grace to be a peacemaker. Being pure of heart may at times seem utterly unattainable. There may even be some among us who do not mourn. But every follower of Jesus will face persecution at some level, and these first followers of Jesus would know it in its bloodiest form. He gave us this last blessing as a candle in the darkness to cling to when all hope seems lost: Whatever we may suffer here, we will rejoice in heaven.

In contrast to the familiar Beatitudes of Matthew, Luke's are more earthy, more responsive to people's current needs. Luke was deeply concerned with social justice, and the picture he paints here is not of Jesus challenging the self-satisfied but of Jesus consoling the suffering. He looked at hungry, weeping, rejected paupers, and told them: *This pain will not last. You will laugh, you will eat, you will have your reward.* He even told people to rejoice over being persecuted because they knew that they were suffering for him.

Does this mean that all poor people are going to heaven? Of course not, though holiness is decidedly more difficult when you live in comfort and don't realize how much you rely on God. Jesus was promising those who suffer that their Mk 10:23
suffering has meaning, that when offered to the Father it can bear fruit in this world and in the world to come.

This might have seemed like nothing but pie-in-the-sky promises made to the suffering until Jesus turned the Beatitudes around and pronounced woe. Woe to the rich, woe Lk 6:24–26
to those who are full, woe to those who laugh, woe to those who are respected. Nobody could write Jesus off as a benevolent wandering philosopher — he was making some enemies,

both in the past and now, two thousand years later, as we read this passage again. How dare he make such threats against hard-working people who have earned their mansions?

There are a number of ways of looking at this. One is a very straightforward understanding that followers of Jesus who have not suffered are at a disadvantage when they do suffer, as they are unprepared for it. The people Jesus was talking to were going to live through persecution and even the destruction of Jerusalem and the enslavement of the Jewish people. Though tragic for anyone, suffering is often more bearable for those who have never had an easy life.

But we can't discount the threat being posed here by the Savior: Woe to you if you are rich, if you are filled, if you laugh, if all speak well of you. Experiencing the good things in this life leaves us little to offer up, little redemptive suffering. It can deafen us to the cry of the poor and the voice of the Lord. There have been canonized saints who suffered little and whose coffers were full, but they are few and far between. It takes incredible virtue to be holy and rich. It's possible, but wealth and comfort are dangerous things — as Jesus warns here — not only because they can anesthetize us to our need for God but also because, in this world where
Mt 26:11 the poor are always with us, our wealth always — *always* —
Jas 5:1–5 comes at somebody's expense. Though the Beatitudes may seem like mere platitudes to those of us who have heard them all our lives, Luke's woes leave us with a reminder that even the most comforting of the Beatitudes must also be convicting. Holiness is costly, after all.

29. The Sermon on the Mount Continued: *Matthew 5:13—7:29*; Luke 6:27–49; 12:13, 22–33; 16:17

After entreating his disciples to be witnesses, to be light to the world, Jesus began to get specific about what it means to follow him. Much of the Sermon on the Mount is a reiteration of the truths handed down in the Old Testament; Jesus was calling Israel back to the moral code enjoined upon them from the beginning. But his relationship to the law was a complicated one. He obeyed the law and all its commands, saying that "until heaven and earth pass away, not the smallest letter or the smallest part of a letter will pass from the law, until all things have taken place." Still, there are elements of the Old Covenant that are not binding for Christians. How can we understand this?

Jesus told us that he came to fulfill the law; in his life he
was perfectly faithful to the law, and in his death he fulfilled
it, saying, "It is finished" or "It is accomplished." In that Jn 19:30
moment, his sacrifice brought us into the New Covenant
and, in a sense, back to Sinai, to the heart of the covenant in Ex 19—24
which God took his people to be his bride. In this New Covenant, in which the Spirit dwells in our heart, the ritual laws that inserted God into everyday life are no longer necessary.

But the moral laws of the Torah are still binding, and Jesus went on to raise the stakes. While Christians living after
the Resurrection could eat pork, they weren't free to commit Mk 7:18–19; Acts
adultery. Indeed, they weren't permitted to entertain lustful 10:13–16
thoughts, even if they never acted on them. Six times in the Sermon on the Mount, Jesus used the formula, "You have heard that it was said. … But I say to you." Each time, he was citing the Mosaic law and elevating it.

Some of these instances are in keeping with the prophetic tradition of developing laws in accord with divine
principles. The prohibition against lust, for example, doesn't
negate the Mosaic command not to commit adultery. At Ex 20:14
other times, Jesus was doing something radical: presenting himself as the new Moses, the one by whose standard all men will be judged. To set oneself up in opposition to the words of Moses was blasphemy, but Jesus didn't think twice about
it. Jesus acknowledged that Moses allowed divorce; then, he Mt 5:31–32;
forbade it. 19:8–9

We must imagine a priest repeatedly saying, "Jesus was wrong about serving the poor. Jesus was wrong about purity." It would have been shocking and infuriating, and yet Jesus spoke with such wisdom and authority that (here, at least) we hear nothing of people storming off in outrage. Because as demanding as Jesus' teaching is, it also speaks to the hunger of our hearts. *Don't hate each other. Don't be cruel. Don't lust after one another. Don't run out on your wife. Don't profane the things of God. Don't fight. Don't loathe.* These ideals make us sit up straighter and wonder if it's really possible to live this way.

For fallen human beings, it's not. But with God's grace, we can be pure and merciful and meek and truthful. Jesus gave us the example and sent his Spirit to fuel our attempts at perfection — and to forgive us when we fail.

Throughout this sermon, Jesus gave us a powerful explanation of what it is to be meek, particularly when he spoke about how we ought to respond to our enemies. When he asked us to submit to blows and robbery (as he would during
Mt 26:67; 27:35 his passion), he described what sounds like a cowardly man, one too weak to resist ill treatment. But there's a difference between submitting out of fear and submitting out of love. When a strong man allows himself to be slapped without fighting back, the assailant has to wonder why. The kind of radical love for our enemies that makes it possible for us to accept such behavior is a more powerful testimony to the love of Jesus Christ than any witness talk or sanitized social life. When we love Jesus and our enemies so much that we keep our anger in check and choose to submit to indignities, we are preaching the Gospel.

There may be evidence of this in the fact that it wasn't
Mt 8:5–13 unheard of for a Roman soldier to approach Jesus, a wandering preacher of the sort that would generally be beneath a soldier's notice. But Jesus loved so radically that everyone noticed. Even soldiers were drawn to him, just as they ought to have been drawn to anyone who tried to live like him. Here, Jesus told his followers that if someone pressed them into service for a mile, they ought to go two. Roman soldiers in Palestine had the right to conscript the locals into carrying a burden. Certainly, such service would usually have been rendered without much good will. But Jesus told them to do twice what was demanded of them and to do it without

bitterness. Is it possible that any of his followers actually did it? Such radical generosity must have seemed almost miraculous. It opened the hearts of pagan soldiers and ultimately changed the world. How can we do the same, refusing bitterness and resentment in favor of life-altering charity?

It is important to point out that Jesus was describing isolated events, not systematic patterns of abuse. This passage has been used to convince Christians that they ought to submit to abusive relationships or tyrannical rulers, when Jesus said nothing here about an ongoing situation of abuse or injustice. The precept not to resort to violence may remain, but a person is absolutely free to leave a situation that is dangerous or to work for change when human dignity is undermined, as Christians have from the very beginning.

Still, the requirement to love our enemies is unchanged, even when that enemy has done unspeakable things. As with many challenges of the Gospel, this may be humanly impossible, but "for God all things are possible." It's helpful to Mt 19:26
remember that love is not a feeling but a choice. When we choose to will the good of those who have hurt us, when we pray for those who have done evil to us, we imitate our Savior who prayed for those who nailed him to the cross. Lk 23:34

The teachings contained in the Sermon on the Mount would take an entire book to discuss adequately. Some are considered elsewhere in this work. Jesus would summarize them all later when he was asked the greatest commandment: "You shall love the Lord, your God, with all your heart, with all your soul, and with all your mind" and "You shall love your neighbor as yourself." Mt 22:37–39
The purpose of the Sermon on the Mount was to flesh out those two commandments; everything contained in the ministry of Jesus is a matter of love. Everything the Church teaches is rooted in the love of God and his desire that we love him and one another. When we encounter something in Scripture or in Church teaching that sounds harsh or cruel or illogical, the question we ask must always be: How does this reflect the love of God? It may take some serious reflection, but the answer is always

there.

Though we can't discuss each point in detail here, we would all do well to meditate deeply on the Sermon on the Mount, asking ourselves if we are living each line so well that it might be read at our funeral. If not, our response should never be discouragement, but prayer and focus: "This week, I ask for the grace not to retaliate, not to ridicule, not to judge. Lord, make me a saint."

Jesus ended his sermon with a strong warning that claiming his name is not enough if we refuse to act as he calls us to act. Even prophecy and exorcism are nothing in the face of our refusal to seek true holiness. He has told us not to judge, not to boast, not to presume. And though people may want to summarize Jesus' teaching as the words of a friendly, indulgent prophet who told people, "Stop judging," a careful reading of the Sermon on the Mount reveals frequent references to sin and hell. Those who claim the name of Jesus and refuse even to attempt to live according to his example will hear him say, "I never knew you." God forbid that we should be among them. We pray for the grace to follow and to repent.

Those of us who do just that will find ourselves like
the wise man who built his house on the rock, a phrase that
likely reminded Jesus' listeners of King Solomon, the king
1 Kgs 6:1 who built the Temple on its mount in Jerusalem. If we build
our lives on Jesus — the cornerstone laid by the Father, the
Is 28:16; stone rejected by the builders — we will become like the
Ps 118:22; great King Solomon before his fall. This sermon that began
Mt 21:42 by telling us how to enter the kingdom — through poverty
in spirit and persecution — now ends by telling us how to
become kings: by following Jesus. Jesus offered two choices:
Obey and become royalty in God's house or turn from God
and find ruin instead.

The crowds who listened were astonished — perhaps the word would be better translated *alarmed*. Jesus spoke as though his word supplanted the Torah, as though he was the divine lawgiver. More disconcertingly, the people believed it.

They didn't know yet who he was or even who he was claiming to be, but though he corrected Moses time and again, they didn't cry out against the apparent blasphemy or even walk away. There was something in his voice, something of unceasing love and unmitigated authority, that kept Pharisee and prostitute alike hushed before him. There was something in his eyes that made them want to follow.

30. The Healing of a Leper: Matthew 8:1–4; *Mark 1:40–45*; Luke 5:12–16

As Jesus, surrounded by these thunderstruck crowds, came down from the mountain, a man suffering from leprosy approached. When we read this story, we tend to think nothing of it; plenty of people approached Jesus to ask for healing. But a leper is a special case. This particular leper may or may not have had Hansen's disease, which is often called "modern leprosy"; the Old Testament description of leprosy included any number of skin conditions, from eczema to
fungal infections to boils. But modern leprosy was not un- Lv 13
known in Israel at the time of Jesus, and its advent in the region a few centuries earlier would certainly have reaffirmed the cultural taboo against those with skin ailments, this one being an especially horrific manifestation of the symptoms described in Leviticus. Those afflicted with leprosy of any
sort were barred from the company of those without leprosy, Lv 13:46; Nm 5:2
but this particular manifestation of the disease was horrifying and disfiguring, leading to isolation that lasted the rest of the sick person's short, miserable life. Lepers were completely shunned by Jewish society, unclean as long as their leprosy persisted and forced to live apart from the rest of the community. On the rare occasion that they saw people without Lv 13:46
leprosy, they were required to call out, "Unclean, unclean," Lv 13:45
as a warning to others and a reminder to themselves of just who they were: the most wretched of outcasts.

For a leper to walk up to Jesus, then, was a great risk. This leper might have been stoned by the crowds, who were terrified lest he touch them and pass on his disease and its attendant isolation. But his need for healing made him brave. And again, there was something about Jesus that made him seem safe. This man was sure that if he threw himself on the mercy of the Master, he wouldn't be banished in disgust. His faith in Jesus' ability to heal is beautiful but not terribly impressive given the many miracles already recounted by the evangelists; his conviction that Jesus would *want* to heal him is something else entirely, speaking volumes about the character of this humble teacher who silenced the powerful but empowered the marginalized to speak.

And so the man knelt before Jesus. "Lord, if you wish, you can make me clean."

What faith! He didn't ask for healing. He didn't technically ask for anything. He just professed his certainty that Jesus could cleanse him — not that Jesus could pray that he be cleansed, but that Jesus could do it himself. And note that his concern here was with being made clean, being restored to communion and permitted to worship in the Temple again. You and I might expect him to want an end to his physical suffering, but the pain of isolation was far worse than the pain of his horrific disease. He wanted community.

Jesus stretched out his hand and touched the man.

It may have been years since he had last been touched. Surely the crowd cringed when Jesus did this unspeakable thing. But while impurity was considered contagious, the all-holy couldn't be defiled. Jesus was so pure that his touch cleansed. When he touched the leprous man, he did more than heal the man's leprosy; he restored the man's humanity in a world that had robbed him of his dignity.

But the leprosy, too, was healed at a mere word from Jesus. It was tangibly healed, in that moment. Did his amputated fingers grow back? Was his missing nose restored? Was his skin suddenly healthy again? Surely if his healing hadn't been evident, people would have objected to Jesus touching a leper, as they later objected to his claim to forgive the para-
Mk 2:1–12 lytic's sins. But there's no record of that, nor even an account of their objection to the man's request.

The crowds were actually remarkably accepting this time around. After all, the leper had asked Jesus to make him clean, something that only a priest could do. He recognized the priesthood of Jesus, at some level, and the crowds (still in awe at what they'd just heard on the mountain) didn't object. Still, Jesus insisted that his followers be faithful to the law as long as it reigned — that is, until he established the New Covenant in his blood. More than this, Jesus knew that it wasn't enough merely for the man to show evidence of having been healed. In order to be received back into the community, his healing had to be verified by a Levitical priest. Until then, he would continue to be an outcast. Jesus was concerned, as always, with the health of a person's heart and soul as well as his body.

Lk 22:20

Lv 14:20

Characteristically, Jesus told the man not to spread about the news of his healing, despite the crowds that surrounded them. This Messianic Secret was sometimes enjoined on people to protect Jesus from being killed before his hour had come. At other times, he was trying to prevent people from getting the wrong idea of what sort of Messiah he was or from following him just to catch a good show. Here it seems that Jesus' reticence was very practical: He wanted the freedom to move about, preaching and healing without hordes of people hindering his movement. When the man spread the news abroad anyway, overjoyed at being restored to his community and healed of his illness, the crowds that thronged to Jesus became so thick that it was impossible for him to preach or heal or even to enter a town openly.

The former leper's disobedience may have been well-intended, but he hindered the preaching of the Gospel by ignoring God's call. Sometimes Jesus told people to speak of what he had done for them; other times he insisted that they be silent. Sometimes he told people to follow him; other times he sent them back to their families. Jesus knew the particular needs of each individual and of each community. Our vocation rests not in doing what we think we ought to do but in doing what he calls us to do, whether or not it's flashy and impressive. Obedience is greater than sacrifice.

Mk 5:19

Mk 7:36; Jn 1:43; Mt 9:9

1 Sm 15:22

Chapter Ten

Calling to Samaritans and Gentiles

31. The Woman at the Well: John 4:4–42

There are moments in the life of Jesus that discomfit his disciples while sailing right over the heads of contemporary readers. Many of these are tied up with his insistence on
treating people like people. Even women. Even Gentiles. Lk 7:32–50; Lk 7:1–10
Even public sinners. The polite thing to do was to ignore Jn 8:1–11
such people, though one could be forgiven for expressing a certain amount of disdain for them. But no matter who he encountered, Jesus looked past the sin or the race or the gender and saw his beloved.

This is particularly striking in his treatment of Samaritans. In our culture, the word *Samaritan* is most associated with the adjective *good*. Yet in order to understand anything about Jesus' interactions with Samaritans, we have to understand first and foremost that the Samaritans and the Jews loathed each other. And by the time of Christ, they had loathed each other for centuries.

At one time, the two groups had all been the nation of Israel, but David's kingdom hadn't lasted very long, and by the time his grandson Rehoboam took the throne, it was already beginning to divide. Jeroboam stole the ten northern 1 Kgs 12:16–20

tribes away, making his capital in Samaria, while the Davidic king ruled over Judah and Benjamin alone (the Southern Kingdom, which came to be known as Judah). In order to prevent his people from going to Jerusalem in the Southern
1 Kgs 12:26–32 Kingdom to worship, Jeroboam set up two new shrines —
Dt 12:13–14 contrary to the law of God — which quickly led his people into idolatry. A few hundred years later, the Northern Kingdom (Israel) was conquered by Assyria, and many of
2 Kgs 17:1–6 her people were deported. The Assyrians brought in pagans to replace the people of Israel so that the land could still
2 Kgs 17:24–41 be worked. The pagans (who worshipped the gods of their homes as well as the God of Israel) intermarried with the Israelites; their descendants were the Samaritans, who had fallen so far as to block the rebuilding of the Temple after the
Ezr 4:1–16 Babylonian Captivity and ultimately to rename their own temple in honor of Zeus. In short, the Samaritans were the older brothers of the Jews, who had turned their backs on their God and worshipped false gods while still considering themselves God's chosen people.

Because of all this, Jews tended to view Samaritans with loathing, much the way we might feel about a once-beloved brother who had deliberately and repeatedly shamed our family while actively trying to ruin our lives. When at all possible, the two groups had nothing to do with each other.
Jn 8:48 Indeed, when Jesus is later accused of being a Samaritan, it's clearly intended as a slur.

This is the backdrop for Jesus' encounter with the Samaritan woman at the well. Even his presence in Samaritan territory was unusual. John says that Jesus "had to pass through Samaria," but Jews often took another route to avoid spending time in that defiled land. Jesus' necessity wasn't a geographical one, but a personal one: He was looking for this woman (known to tradition as Saint Photina). For this one lost sheep, he had to bridge the divide between Jew and Samaritan — and, ultimately, for every Samaritan and every lost and forsaken person who would read this story and feel hope again.

Jesus made his way into town and sent his disciples ahead to buy food, staying behind to pray, or (perhaps) to meet a woman he knew would be coming. It was the middle of the day, the sun high in the sky, and not a time for great activity around the well; women would come to draw water in the cool of the morning or of the evening, not at noon. At noon, the well was generally frequented only by those who were trying to avoid the sneers and the snide remarks of a town that had turned against them.

Jesus was thirsty, but though the disciples likely carried some sort of bucket, he hadn't asked them to leave it. He wanted to need help, to be at the mercy of someone who was convinced she wasn't worth anything. As Jesus sat there, tired from his journey, Photina approached.

The setting would certainly have put John's readers in mind of a wedding. Abraham's servant had found Isaac's bride
beside a well, as Jacob had found Rachel, and Moses found Gn 24; 29
Zipporah. To the reader of Scripture who has been steeped in Ex 2:15–21
the stories of the Torah, this is obviously the beginning of a betrothal. And yet the only things we know about this woman are that she was a Samaritan and that she avoided the company of other women by coming to the well at midday, suggesting that she was an outcast. Certainly, she wasn't the ideal spouse for one such as Jesus, even if he had been planning to marry.

Nor did he treat her the way a suitor would. No pleasantries were exchanged, though that comes as no surprise. One would expect a Jewish man in the first century to ignore a strange woman he met in public, and particularly a Samaritan woman. But Jesus addressed her: "Give me a drink."

When we first pay attention to the beginning of this exchange, we're startled by its abruptness. It genuinely seems rude. And while there's no expectation of excessive courtesy in a situation without any real precedent, it's worth close con-
sideration. Jesus treated outcasts with dignity, but his first Mk 2:16; 5:25–34;
address to this woman was demanding, almost as though he Lk 7:36–50
saw her as a means to an end.

Is it possible that he did this deliberately? Perhaps Photina had spent her life bowing and scraping before people who treated her like filth. She'd built walls to protect herself from their ugliness. Had Jesus treated her courteously, those walls might have stayed in place. She would have quietly given him his drink and moved on. Instead, Jesus pushed on her broken places. He probed her wounds so that she snapped at him.

"How can you, a Jew, ask me, a Samaritan woman, for a drink?" With that outburst, her walls were down. Our God, who is usually such a gentleman, had lanced her wounds in order to bring healing.

Jesus' answer was enigmatic, as was so often the case. "If you knew the gift of God and who is saying to you, 'Give me a drink,'" he said, "you would have asked him and he would have given you living water." He almost seems to have been reassuring her that he wasn't there to use her, like everyone else in her life. He was there to give. And perhaps something in his voice touched her stony heart. Is there a note of hope in her next question? Or was it mere derision, pointing out how impossible his claim was? "Sir, you do not even have a bucket."

Over and again, Jesus repeated the word *give*, now offering living water that will satisfy all thirst forever — living
Jer 2:13 water of which only God could be the source. To a woman
who had grown accustomed to being used, he promised
something that was pure gift: the Spirit that wells up within
Jn 6:63 us and gives us new life. And, possibly for the first time in
many years, Photina allowed herself to hope.

It's worth taking a moment to wonder at her response to this promise of living water. If we put aside our expectation that all Jesus' words are poetic and meaningful, we can be honest. Without context, he sounded like a madman, babbling about his ability to give unceasing water without even having access to a bucket. There's no reason Photina ought to have believed him. But there was something in his eyes, something in his voice that compelled her. He spoke words that ought to have been nonsense, but they penetrated the walls surrounding her heart, and she responded with utter faith. Rather than roll her eyes and walk away when a man without a bucket promised miraculous, unceasing water, she believed. "Sir, give me this water, so that I may not be thirsty or have to keep coming here to draw water."

Give me this water so that I can further retreat into myself, hiding from the knowing eyes and wagging tongues that follow me wherever I walk. Please, Lord, she prayed, *I just want some peace.*

But Jesus wasn't offering her an easy way out of her suffering. He was offering her the opportunity to know and be known, to be fully loved, to be his. And in order to do that, he had to call out her brokenness and bring true healing. So he looked into her eyes, brimming with hope, and broke her heart. He was offering her grace beyond all measure, but in order to be filled with that grace, she first had to let him into the shameful places of her life.

"Go call your husband," he said, and she knew that this exchange, like every other exchange in her life, would end in her shame.

"I do not have a husband," she muttered, already turning to walk away. He had shone a spotlight on the one thing in her life that made her feel ineligible for love.

"You are right in saying, 'I do not have a husband,'" he said softly. "For you have had five husbands, and the one you have now is not your husband. What you have said is true."

Nobody likes having her past thrown in her face, and Photina must have flinched when he first spoke these shameful words. This was, after all, the reason she was at the well alone in the middle of the day: to avoid the cruel gossips who called her cursed or unlovable for her husbands' deaths or disappearances or affairs. The Gospel is unclear as to why Photina had been with so many men. Though she's commonly depicted as a serial adulteress, it's unlikely in that culture that a woman would be able to marry so many times if each divorce had been entirely her fault — if indeed she was divorced and not many times widowed. But the details may be vague so that we can see ourselves in Photina whether our

misfortune is entirely of our own making or not our fault at
Tb 3:7–10 all. Whatever the reason for her multiple marriages, Jesus
loved her just the same.

It took a moment for Photina to recognize that Jesus' words had no judgment in them. But then she realized — he was new in town and a Jew; nobody would have told him these things about her. He had read her heart. He had seen every ugly thing she'd done and every thing that had been done to her. And still he spoke to her. Still he offered her living water. He knew who she was and he still wanted her.

More than that, he offered her himself. The man she
was living with was her sixth, the number of imperfection,
falling just short of the covenant number seven. Now the
bridegroom stood before her, a woman encountered at a well,
and offered to become the seventh, the number of perfection,
Gn 2:3; Lv 25:4, the number of the covenant, the number whose very root in
8–10; Jos 6:2–5 Hebrew is the word *oath*.

It was too much for her, this tender offer of healing, this
insistence on treating her brokenness. She pulled back, looking
for a diversion. Like so many of us when Jesus is asking
more than we're prepared to give, Photina switched from relationship
to theory, from intimacy to ideology: "Our ances-
Gn 33:18–20 tors worshipped on this mountain, but you people say that
the place to worship is in Jerusalem."

Jesus didn't take the bait. He wasn't willing to fight her.
Dt 12:13–14 He just spoke the truth (blasphemous to both Jew and Samaritan)
that God was about to do something new, inviting
people to worship anywhere as long as they were worshipping
in Spirit and truth.

This idea was more than Photina could accept, so she issued what can only be read as a dismissal: "I know that the Messiah is coming, the one called the Anointed; when he comes, he will tell us everything." *It's been great chatting with you, but I really do need to get going.*

Then, for the first time — and the only time until his
Mk 14:61–62 trial — Jesus claimed the title of Messiah. To the outcast of
the outcasts of the outcasts: a disdained and despised Sa-

maritan woman. Because she was worthy of intimacy.

Something must have happened then, some intense gaze or deep stirring of the soul. Because when the disciples returned a moment later, Photina was no longer interested in walking away. Instead, she ran back to the town to tell everybody about Jesus. She left her water jar behind, abandoning her previous purpose, and went straight to the people she had every right to hate. She gave her testimony: "Come see a man who told me everything I have done. Could he possibly be the Messiah?" To the people who had made her life hell, she brought the Good News of the Gospel. Because her healing had made her a fount of mercy.

The disciples didn't ask Jesus why he was doing such a shocking thing as speaking with a Samaritan woman; at this point, they had become accustomed to his flouting of social norms. They just wanted him to eat. But Jesus refused: "My food is to do the will of the one who sent me and to finish his work." Jesus did eat, fully human as he was. But he hungered far more to do the Father's will.

Truly, he hungered for the hearts of the Samaritan people. Though he had come to Samaria just for Photina, she also represented all of Samaria. The Gentiles who had been brought in to occupy Samaria had worshipped five different sets of pagan gods (the "five husbands" of the woman 2 Kgs 17:29–31
at the well), and though they paid lip service to the God of Israel, they didn't worship him in spirit and truth ("the one you have now is not your husband"). When Jesus came to espouse Photina, he was inviting the Samaritans who had turned from God's covenant back into relationship with him. He was offering himself as their bridegroom, just as he was the bridegroom of Judah and, ultimately, of all believers, Jew and Gentile alike.

Meanwhile the Samaritans were beginning to approach, convicted by Photina's testimony. Though broken, she had become a missionary; indeed, it was only because she was broken that she'd been able to hear Jesus' call in the first place. Her encounter with Jesus' love, the mercy he had offered her when everybody else just sat in judgment — these things changed not only her but also the people of her village, who saw a light in her eyes that they hadn't seen in years, who heard her speak without shame or regret or pain because somehow the man at the well had redeemed her past. And so Samaritans sat down with Jews, like brothers. It was the beginning of Jesus' call to the ten northern tribes to come home. The laughing and rejoicing around those tables must have been a sight to see for the two short days that Jesus stayed in Sychar, something of a family reunion when everybody had thought the feud was irreparable.

And though the Samaritans who came to know Jesus read only the Samaritan Pentateuch (very similar to the Pentateuch Jews and Christians share) and had no Messianic psalms to read, nor prophecies of Isaiah, they saw in Jesus
Dt 18:15 the prophet foretold by Moses. They heard him preach and
spoke to him individually, and they, too, came to believe, in
fulfillment of Ezekiel's prophecy that Israel and Judah would
Ez 37:21–22 be reconciled and the lost tribes restored to the Father. "We
have heard for ourselves, and we know that this is truly the
savior of the world." The word *savior* was not an uncommon
term for rulers, meaning the one who delivered a people from
Jgs 3:9, 15 their enemies. The Samaritans were proclaiming Jesus king
of all the world, not merely of Judea and Samaria, but they
hit upon the further truth that he would save the world from
sin and death.

Jesus was not only Messiah but also Savior; the fact that this truth was first proclaimed by Samaritans further shows the boundless love of the God who rejects nobody. Pagans and Samaritans are invited into the kingdom. Women and sinners take leading roles. And as Jesus returned to Galilee, he left behind him a community of believers from whom we never hear again (unless this town was the home of the Samaritan leper we will meet in Luke 17:11–19, but that's nothing more than speculation). Though tradition tells us that Photina went on to be martyred for her faith in Jesus, we can't know if the others in her village continued to follow, or what the death and resurrection of Christ did to their faith. All we can know for sure is that Jesus had touched the hearts of these Samaritans, and that's not the kind of thing one forgets easily.

32. Healing of the Centurion's Servant: *Matthew 8:5–13*; Luke 7:1–10; (John 4:46–54)

As Jesus traveled the countryside preaching and healing, his reputation continued to grow. It's no great surprise that the occupying forces heard about a man who gathered large crowds everywhere he went. The Romans must have been careful to keep tabs on Jesus, both where he went and what he said. But language like "kingdom of heaven" and "Son of Man" meant very little to those without a Jewish background. All they could see was that this man was something of a philosopher, so they let him alone.

There were some, however, who listened more intently to the wild stories that were being passed about, stories of remarkable healings. One centurion found himself beginning to believe that this ragged young Jew had power like he had never seen before. So when a certain slave of his fell ill and was suffering terribly, the centurion turned to Jesus for help.

In the New American Bible, we're told that the slave was "valuable" to the centurion, but the word might also be translated "precious" or "dear." When viewed through the lens of American chattel slavery, it's hard to imagine a slave whose financial worth was so great that a Roman centurion would be willing to be debased in order to secure that slave's health. But this ancient form of slavery is clearly something distinct from the inherently dehumanizing practice whose repercussions are still felt today. (Ex 20:10; 21:2; Dt 23:16–17) The centurion's servant was precious to him, a companion so dear that he didn't think twice about becoming a supplicant before a penniless Jew on his slave's behalf. The ability to love his servants may have humanized this centurion in the eyes of the Jews even more than his financial contributions to the community.

Either way, this soldier must have been a remarkable

man. He was a leader in the army of their pagan enemy, and yet the Jews described him as one who loved their nation. He
Jn 6:59 was a Gentile, but he'd built the synagogue in Capernaum. And he believed in Jesus.

When Jesus was told of the situation, he was perfectly willing to take the time to visit the servant and heal him. But the remarkable Roman knew that Jesus didn't need incense or incantations or the power of his charismatic personality to effect healing. He could speak the word, and it would be done.

Knowing that such a thing was possible, the centurion didn't think it right to ask Jesus to go out of his way. Perhaps he was also aware that Jews who entered Gentile homes could
Acts 10:28 become ritually unclean. Certainly, he had deep respect for the Nazarene, though the centurion was a Roman military commander who would have been within his rights to order any common Jew around.

So rather than summoning Jesus to his home, he made his unforgettable statement of faith: "Lord, I am not worthy that you should enter under my roof. But say the word and let my servant be healed." What a thing for a centurion to say! He spoke as though he knew that Jesus was a king. Certainly, he knew that Jesus had the power to do whatever he chose, natural or supernatural; the natural world obeyed the commands of Jesus just as surely as the centurion's soldiers obeyed his commands.

Even Jesus was amazed to hear such a statement. The word used here to describe Jesus' astonishment at the cen-
Mt 8:27; 15:31; turion's faith appears repeatedly in Scripture to describe the
27:14 reaction of the crowds, the disciples, and even Pontius Pilate. But it's used of Jesus only twice: in this encounter, when he marveled at a pagan's faith in him, and when he marveled
Mk 6:6 at Nazareth's lack of faith. The centurion had no good reason to believe in him; Nazareth had every reason to suspect that there was something special about him. But the centurion believed, and Jesus' former neighbors did not. How this man's confidence and selflessness must have consoled Jesus,

especially when so many of his people were unwilling to believe. How full his heart must have been to see how this man trusted him so completely.

So the story would go again and again, as prostitutes flocked to Jesus while the priests and scribes turned up their
noses, as faithful Jews cried out for his blood while pagans Mt 27:25
called him the Son of God. Later in the Gospels, as well as Mt 27:54
throughout Acts, the pattern would continue. Though many Jews accepted Jesus, far more did not. But Gentiles did, from east to west. Jesus looked on this Gentile centurion in particular and marveled. Nowhere in Israel had Jesus found such faith, faith that viewed him as King of Israel and all creation. For the people of Israel who failed to believe, on the other hand, Jesus sadly foretold that "the children of the kingdom will be driven out into the outer darkness, where there will be wailing and grinding of teeth." While this assertion sounds like a threat, it's more of a lament. Jesus rejoiced that the Gentiles would enter into the promise, but he grieved those of his people who would refuse him.

The centurion certainly had great faith. But one wonders if his reluctance to inconvenience Jesus by having him come all the way to his house was entirely about true humility. Is it possible that he just felt he wasn't worth suffering for? Even if that wasn't the centurion's motivation, it's often ours. We turn from God not because we want a life without him, but because we're convinced that he couldn't possibly want us. Healthy guilt that ought to drive us to repentance turns into shame and self-loathing.

But when we're honest with ourselves, when we acknowledge that we're afraid that Jesus doesn't want us but still we come to him just the same, he is as pleased as he was by the centurion's faith, and as eager to give us what we need. By God's grace, may "Lord, I am not worthy" never become "Lord, you couldn't possibly love me." But if it does, let him say the word and heal our troubled souls.

The actual healing in this story almost seems an afterthought. The real miracle is the faith of the centurion. And with that act of faith, the words of a pagan enemy of Israel were placed on the lips of billions of Catholics for centuries to come. We, too, know ourselves to be unworthy of the gift of the Eucharist. *But still, God, please. Heal me. Make me worthy.*

Chapter Eleven

Followers Drawn to a Healer

33. The Would-be Followers of Jesus: Matthew 8:16–22; *Luke 9:57–62*

The Gospels record in detail some thirty-five miracles worked by Jesus, but it's clear that these were only the beginning. Frequently, when there's a transition from one place to another, the evangelists use some variation of the formula "Jesus went about the country curing the sick and casting out demons." He may have worked hundreds, even thousands of miracles during his public ministry.

Mt 4:23; 8:16; 9:35; 15:30; Mk 1:34, 39; Lk 4:40

As Matthew alludes to these healings and exorcisms, he uses Isaiah 53, a song about God's suffering servant who would be "pierced for our sins, / crushed for our iniquity." From the earliest days of the Church, Christians have seen this passage as a prophecy of the passion of Christ. The suffering servant, Isaiah said, would take away the sins of many and win pardon for their offenses by surrendering himself to death. Matthew references the passage here not in connection to the saving work of Christ on the cross, but as a prediction of Jesus' healing ministry: "He took away our infirmities / and bore our diseases." Jesus didn't come just to save us from damnation but to bring healing to our wounded souls and to speak the love of the Father to our

Is 53:5

Lk 22:37; Acts 8:29–35; 1 Pt 2:22–25

Is 53:12

hearts. He didn't just come to heal *their* infirmities, but *ours* as well. And if we look to the source text in Isaiah, we see Hebrew words that could be rendered "griefs" and "sorrows" as well as "infirmities" and "diseases." This Jesus cares not only for our debilitating diseases but also for our nagging sorrows, not only for our disabling wounds but for our long-hidden griefs. How astonishing that he cares.

These miracles of healing and liberation serve as evidence of Jesus' divine appointment, but they're not just proofs. Jesus doesn't use the sick to make a point. Each miracle is an encounter with an individual, each far less about the repair of a body than about the salvation of a soul. Jesus was proclaiming liberation from sin and death as a free gift to the whole human race, but he was also offering peace and joy to each person he met. He's the savior of mankind and the savior of each man, the redeemer of the world and the one who has delighted in the very idea of you since before there was time.

For some, the spectacle of the miracles was enough to make them want to follow Jesus, to seek a real relationship that went deeper than their initial enthusiasm over the supernatural phenomena they'd witnessed. Others heard Jesus preach and knew they would never be the same. For a third group, there had been a personal encounter that wasn't about wisdom or power but just about the man himself — the compassion in his eyes, perhaps, or the peace that radiated from him. Whatever their motivation, people regularly asked to follow Jesus.

On one occasion, Jesus was attempting to avoid the crowds when a scribe approached, an educated man well-versed in the law, one of that class that would largely oppose Jesus as he came to the end of his life. But this man was convicted. "Teacher, I will follow you wherever you go," he said.

It was a good sentiment, though addressing Jesus as "teacher" doesn't demonstrate much of an idea of who he truly was. Still, to hear such a thing from a scribe must have been remarkable. But Jesus cautioned this man, used to some degree of comfort and stability: "Foxes have dens and birds of the sky have nests, but the Son of Man has nowhere to rest his head."

There's something almost wistful in this moment. He's warning the scribe, of course, of the difficulties of following him. But is he also expressing his own longing for a home? It's natural to the human person to belong somewhere, to be known. Even more so for God, who is fully known by the other persons of the Trinity. But we who are born twisted by original sin live in exile, far from our true heavenly home. Though we may live in the same place our whole lives, we never truly belong. Though we may sit across the dinner table from the same person for seventy years, no creature can ever fully know another. We are strangers and sojourners, searching for our heavenly home.

Heb 11:13–16;
Eph 2:19;
Gn 23:4

When Jesus walked out of the Holy House in Nazareth and set off on the road to Calvary, he stepped into the homelessness that every human being experiences. He, too, didn't quite belong. He wasn't fully known. The Son of Man who holds galaxies in the palms of his hands became a homeless man. And in wandering as we wander, he taught us not to be vagrants but pilgrims, with our hearts fixed on our true home.

Jesus looked at another man in the crowd and called, with no preamble, "Follow me." The man was taken aback. Yes, he would follow, of course he would follow! He just had a few things to take care of first. He wanted Jesus, but he wanted his old life, too. He only asked to bury his father before following Jesus, which seems like a reasonable request (though James and John had left their father behind at a word from the Lord). But there's no indication that his father had died. He may have been asking to wait a few years, just a few years, until it was a more convenient time.

Mk 1:20

We've all done that. "I'll obey, Lord. Just let me finish my degree." Or see where this relationship goes. Or say this one last ugly thing. Or save up a little more money. Here Jesus shows no patience for that kind of vacillation. "Follow me," he says, "and let the dead bury their dead."

It's shocking enough to read these words in the West
twenty centuries later. For ancient Jews, such a statement
was near blasphemy. Burying the dead was an act of piety so
valuable that the Old Testament hero Tobit risked his life to
Tb 2:3–8 do it. It was so important in Jewish culture that only the high
Lv 21:11; priest or a Nazirite consecrated to the Lord was exempted
Nm 6:6–7 from the obligation to bury his father. All other priests were
Lv 21:1–3 required to bury their immediate relatives. When Jesus told
the man to let the dead bury their dead, he was saying that
following him is a higher call even than the Levitical priesthood.

Finally, someone approached and said, "I will follow you, Lord, but first let me say farewell to my family at home." It's an odd request when Jesus had just told someone not to delay even long enough to bury his father, but we all hope that an exception will be made for us, that maybe we will be allowed to be halfway holy while others are required to give their all.

The man's words were reminiscent of an earlier call,
when the prophet Elijah had thrown his cloak over Elisha.
"Please, let me kiss my father and mother good-bye," Elisha
1 Kgs 19:19–21 had begged, "and I will follow you." In asking to take leave
of his parents, Jesus' would-be disciple was in good company.
But Jesus made it clear that his call was greater than that of
Israel's greatest prophet, too urgent to allow for prolonged
goodbyes or the tying up of loose ends. In following Jesus,
this man would become greater than Elisha, who had a dou-
2 Kgs 2:9–13 ble portion of Elijah's spirit. Such a vocation must necessarily
require sacrifices.

Elisha had been allowed to say goodbye to his parents,
but when he followed, he took the oxen that had been his
livelihood, slaughtered them, broke up his plow, and roasted
1 Kgs 19:19–21 the oxen over its pieces. He followed with abandon, burning every bridge lest he be tempted to go back. This man
approaching Jesus didn't even want to focus on his plow, let
alone break it up as a sacrifice. With his hand on the plow
and his eyes looking back at the life he'd left behind, the fur-
row he plowed would be crooked, his work useless. To follow

Jesus, he had to be willing to fix his eyes on the Lord, not on his sacrifice or desires or plans.

Taken together, these encounters show us just what Jesus requires of his disciples: not merely Sunday Mass attendance or good behavior Saturday night. He isn't seeking nice people; he's making saints. This New Covenant demands not only our attention and our obedience but our very selves, our hearts handed over entirely to the Lord and our eyes fixed only on him.

34. The Calming of the Storm: Matthew 8:23–27; *Mark 4:35–41*; Luke 8:22–25

As if to underline the difficulties one encounters as a disciple of Jesus, Matthew takes us from this conversation directly into a boat on the Sea of Galilee. Jesus and his disciples were crossing the sea, and Jesus took the opportunity to get some rest. As he slept, a storm came up — a storm so violent, Matthew describes it using the word *earthquake*. The same word describes apocalyptic events elsewhere in the Gospels and in Revelation. Mt 24:7; 27:54; Rv 6:12; 8:5

For Matthew, this was more than an ordinary storm. If he wasn't there (Matthew describes his call shortly after this event, while Mark and Luke place it earlier), he certainly heard tell of it from the other apostles, many of whom were lifelong sailors and still shook their heads in wonder at the storm's power. And Jesus slept. The waves were breaking over the boat. It was filling with water. The men were bailing for all they were worth. The skies had opened. The world was ending. And still Jesus slept.

It's a familiar image for most followers of Jesus: We're overwhelmed, frantic, terrified — and God is doing nothing, saying nothing. It's as though he's sleeping.

But he's as close to us as he was to the apostles. They struggled desperately, never once asking him for help. In fairness to them, it was one thing to heal illnesses, another entirely to command the wind and the sea; it couldn't have occurred to them that Jesus had such power. Still, how could he sleep through all this?

Finally, they gave in. Knowing how exhausted he was, they had been hesitant to wake him, but the extremity of the situation left them no choice. "Teacher!" they cried, "Do you not care that we are perishing?"

As an opening statement, it's remarkable. They leveled an accusation at Jesus, rooted in their panic, despite not once having asked for help. Again, we see ourselves in the apostles. We insist on doing things our own way, fighting desperately to make it work, and when we finally have recourse to prayer, we're already angry at God for not having helped us with a situation we hadn't invited him into.

The minor differences between the Gospel accounts can present theologians with some difficulties, but for those who read seeking God, they are an invitation. Did Jesus rebuke the disciples first or the storm? The Gospels don't agree. It's possible that when he first spoke, not everyone heard, whereas all heard what followed the calm that descended. For our purposes, the difference presents an opportunity for reflection: Sometimes in our lives, when we finally get around to asking God for help, he responds immediately and only later invites us to ponder why we may have delayed turning to him. Other times, he lets us sit with the consequences of our pretended self-sufficiency before answering our prayer.

Whether he spoke to the disciples first or not, Jesus certainly spoke to the storm. In fact, he *rebuked* it — a word
Mt 17:18; often used in his dealings with demons. Jesus held the same
Mk 1:25; Lk 4:41 authority over the terrifying powers of the natural world as
over an immaterial unclean spirit. The moment he called out
to the wind and the sea to be still, they did just that.

Ps 65:8; 89:10; Who but God alone could calm such a storm with just
93:4; Sir 39:17 a word? The entire episode was reminiscent of Psalm 107, in
which the Lord "hushed the storm to silence, / the waves of
Ps 107:29 the sea were stilled" after sailors cried out to the Lord. It's no
wonder that the disciples were awestruck, asking, "Who then
is this whom even wind and sea obey?" They were beginning
to get the sense that he was more than a man, more even

than the chosen anointed of God. He spoke with the power of the Creator, and it was done. In the Jewish imagination, the sea symbolized chaos and evil, all the terror of the natural Ps 69:1-3;
world that went unconquered by a people disinclined to sea- Dn 7:2–7
faring. Jesus triumphed over this — over the danger of fathomless deeps and malevolent creatures, over the chaos of the formless sea — with a mere word. Who must he be to wield such power?

This power makes sense of his rebuke of his followers, too. "Why are you terrified?" he asked. One can almost hear a note of disappointment in his voice: *Don't you know me yet? Don't you realize how much I love you? How could I ever let you be hurt? Why didn't you ask for my help?* This isn't to say that he always saves those who love him from suffering, but when we turn to him there is always greater peace afterwards, whether external or internal. The disciples would learn that eventually, as (God willing) will we.

What may be most striking in this narrative is the contrast: Demons obey God's word. The sea obeys God's word. The rain and wind obey God's word. Withered limbs, immune systems, even corpses obey God's word. The only thing that doesn't is the human will. There's some consolation in knowing that even those who walked with him doubted, but we who have two millennia of saints and theologians and mystics to tell us who God is ought to seek to trust him more even than those who walked with him. We, too, have seen miracles. We, too, fail to trust. But, like the disciples, we can always cry out to Jesus. Even if we cry out with anger or despair, he hears our cry. And whether or not he answers our prayer as we would hope, he is always near to those who call to him. Ps 145:18

35. The Healing of the Gerasene Demoniac: Matthew 8:28–34; *Mark 5:1–20*; Luke 8:26–39

After this Jesus went into a Gentile region — the first time the Synoptics tell of the adult Jesus leaving Jewish territory. As he disembarked from the boat in this unclean land, he met a man possessed by unclean spirits and living among the tombs, the most unclean of places. But Jesus didn't shy away from this trifecta of impurity. He entered in and engaged this man who had been living in bondage, though he had broken the chains put on him by his neighbors. He was naked and bloody and must have been terrifying to the disciples as he ran up to Jesus. Perhaps Peter placed himself between Jesus and this perceived threat, as the captive raced up to the Lord while begging Jesus to leave him alone. Both attracted to Jesus and repelled by him, the demoniac stands with all who are trapped by evil or sin, who long for the Lord and are terrified of him at the same time. But however the man pleaded, Jesus loved him too much to leave him alone.

As is often the case, the demons possessing the man rec-
Mk 1:24 ognized Jesus — or, rather, recognized the one who had sent
him. Though the demons use the same title for Jesus that
Lk 1:32 Gabriel did at the annunciation, it's possible that calling Je-
sus "Son of the Most High God" might not exactly have been an acclamation of his divinity, but merely an acknowledgement that Jesus had been commissioned by the God of Israel. Years later, though, a possessed girl would identify Paul and
Acts 16:17 his companions as "slaves of the Most High God," a similar
title with a marked difference in status. Perhaps Jesus' deeds up to this point had begun to set hell trembling and driven Satan to realize just who he had contended with in the desert. Certainly, his minions had begun to be afraid of this wandering miracle-worker. But while the demons who possessed this man begged to be left alone, Jesus continued to drive them out.

Rather than be sent into the abyss, the demons entreated him to drive them into the two thousand swine that were feeding nearby. Jesus consented, knowing that they would drive the swine off the cliff and gain the attention of the swineherds and thus the whole town. And so it happened, the pigs rushing down the bank into the sea in a scene remi-
Ex 14:27 niscent of Pharaoh's army being drowned during the Exodus.

The swineherds were shocked (and likely outraged) and

ran to tell the others about the tragic loss of livestock. The townspeople, for their part, reacted with interest. They left their work behind and went to investigate this story.

But when they saw the demoniac clothed and in his right mind, they were terrified. Pigs might stampede and run off a cliff at some unseen provocation, but the complete healing of a criminally insane man could only be the result of some enormous power. Even the loss of two thousand pigs seemed small compared to a man's changed heart.

Rather than invite Jesus to heal others among them who were sick and possessed, the people begged him to leave. We can only imagine how it pierced his heart each time those he loved with an everlasting love not only turned from him Jer 31:3 but chased him away. But his power was too frightening to be trifled with, whatever benefits it might offer. Again, we can sympathize, we who want the Lord to give us peace and comfort but are terrified lest he truly inflame our hearts and transform our lives.

But it was too late for the demoniac. His heart was already inflamed. He had been healed, yes, but then he had sat at the feet of Jesus, basking in the radiance of the one who had thought he was worth saving even when he was at his lowest. He pleaded with Jesus to take him along. Israel wasn't ready yet for a Gentile apostle, though, so Jesus gave him a different mission: "Go home to your family and announce to them all that the Lord in his pity has done for you."

Giving up everything to follow Jesus might have seemed an easier task than evangelizing his family, one of the most difficult things we're called to do as Christians. But the man accepted his vocation, the only time in Mark that Jesus told anybody to tell people about his healing. With this, the Gerasene demoniac became the first missionary to the Gentiles.

One might think this an odd choice. How could a man so recently considered insane have any credibility when it comes to such proclamations? But his personal testimony to the healing he had experienced made him, like the Samaritan woman, the perfect evangelist. He wasn't speaking about Jn 4:28–30

theory but about his own experience of Jesus. His witness was so compelling that when Jesus later returned to that territory, crowds flocked to him just as they did in Judea and
Mk 7:31—8:9 Galilee. Jesus had told the healed man to announce all that "the Lord" had done for him; the man proclaimed what Jesus had done — Jesus who is Lord.

Thus ends Jesus' sojourn into Gentile territory for the time being. As with the Samaritan woman, he had gone all that way to do one thing. For one human soul, he would gladly cross a small sea. For one human soul, he would travel through "enemy" territory. For one human soul, he would have climbed Calvary, gone to hell and back, made the world new again. One soul is worth everything.

36. The Paralytic Lowered through the Roof: *Matthew 9:1–8*; Mark 2:1–12; Luke 5:17–26

After his time with the Gentiles, Jesus made his way back to Capernaum. It had once been something of a sanctuary for him, but for the rest of his life it would be difficult for Jesus not to draw a crowd. This time there were many Pharisees and teachers of the law there. Up to this point, Jesus had been fairly uncontroversial in his ministry, though he was already rather more pro-Gentile than the people would have
Lk 4:24–27 preferred. Even claiming to inaugurate the kingdom of God
Mk 1:14–15 made him just one of many candidates for the role of Messiah. But from this moment on he began almost needling the religious authorities, deliberately scandalizing them in order to expose their hypocrisy and invite people to seek true union with God through the law rather than contenting themselves with legal minutiae.

Jesus was teaching the crowd when four men approached, carrying their friend on a stretcher. They had heard about Jesus and were sure that if they could get him to speak life over their friend, the paralyzed man would be healed. But the crowds were too thick; people simply couldn't stay away from this Jesus. The men politely asked to pass, then tried to shove and even shouted that they needed to get through, but the people were intent on getting close to Jesus themselves, and these men were not going to make any progress.

Unlike some in the crowd who were mere thrill-seekers, these four were desperate. They had a friend who needed healing, and they would stop at nothing to bring him to the Lord. So they went around to the back of the house. They climbed up onto the roof and began to rip it off as people within gasped in indignation. Then they hoisted their friend up and lowered him down right in front of Jesus.

What audacity! What charity! As they surveyed their work, they must have wondered whether they would be arrested or rewarded with what they sought. Instead, Jesus turned his piercing eyes on their paralyzed friend and said, "Child, your sins are forgiven." Forgiven, the Gospel says, because of *their* faith, because they had fought for him. The power of Christian friendship cannot be overestimated. Look at the miracles God works in response to our intercession.

And yet the men on the roof must have been frustrated, if not furious. If Jesus wanted to go about claiming a ridiculous thing like sins being forgiven, that was his business, but what on earth made him think that's what they were looking for? Obviously, if they brought him a man on a stretcher, they wanted the man to be healed.

The crowd, meanwhile, was appalled, especially the scribes and Pharisees. Who was this man, claiming that he could forgive sins? Who but God alone could forgive sins? They were right, of course — that was exactly Jesus' point.

We don't know what the paralytic himself thought. Perhaps as Jesus had looked into his eyes, he had seen that this man's greatest suffering wasn't his paralysis but his guilt. Maybe the man had thought the best he could hope for was the ability to walk, shoulders stooped under the weight of some great shame, and Jesus had offered him his heart's true desire instead.

Or maybe he was livid. He'd asked God for what he wanted and had been given what he needed instead; we, too, can find God's astonishing mercy infuriating when we think we have better plans.

This time, though, God was offering healing both spiritual and physical. *Ah, you think I don't have the authority to forgive sins? Well, I suppose you can't see evidence of a soul washed clean — at least not right away. But let me prove that I have the power to do what I say, that the Son of Man has authority on earth to forgive sins. My friend, rise, pick up your mat, and go home.*

The man did just that. Glorifying God, he picked up his mat and went home. He wasn't half-healed, staggering along with his arms around his friends' shoulders for support. No, he took up his mat himself and walked all the way home, fully restored. And if he was physically made new, then he was spiritually reborn as well. His sins really had been forgiven.

But though the crowd may have been delighted at this turn of events, there was something percolating in the hearts of those who knew the word of God. Jesus hadn't merely claimed to forgive sins, he had called himself the Son of Man. To our ears, that might sound like a title accenting his humanity, but Jews of his day would have heard an allusion to the Book of Daniel.

Rv 1:13; 14:14 "Son of Man" is the title Jesus used most often to refer
to himself. Nobody else ever used that title for him, except
Saint Stephen at the moment of his martyrdom when he saw
Acts 7:56 Jesus at the right hand of the Father. To our ears it sounds
like an excessively wordy way of saying "man," but those who
heard Jesus speaking knew that while "son of man" often
Nm 23:19; Ps 8:5 meant human, Jesus' use was a reference to the Book of Daniel, where the prophet was given a vision of one like a Son
Dn 7:13 of Man "coming with the clouds of heaven." This language
presents him as divine — only God rides upon the clouds
— but with the appearance of a human being. According
to Daniel, this God-man was then presented to "the Ancient One" or "the Ancient of Days," who is God the Father,
shown as distinct from the Son of Man. The Son of Man
Dn 7:14 was given authority over all peoples and made the ruler of
the everlasting kingdom not made by human hands that had

been foretold earlier in Daniel. Dn 2:34, 44

This second divine figure was baffling to Jewish monotheism, leaving rabbis arguing about who he might be. That it was considered a divine title is evident, though, from the Sanhedrin's response when Jesus used this title before them: They declared him guilty of blasphemy. This was no esoteric Mk 14:61–64 reference to his humanity. Those who heard it knew Jesus was claiming to be far more than a mere man.

Along with the implication that he was Daniel's Son of Man, Jesus was claiming a power clearly reserved to God alone: the authority to forgive sins. Interestingly, Matthew extends that claim beyond Jesus himself, saying that the crowds "glorified God who had given such authority to human beings." For Matthew, there's a clear connection between Jesus' authority to forgive sins and a forgiveness of sins that would be practiced by others in his name: the Sacrament of Reconciliation.

But with all this apparent blasphemy, the story ends with no account of lingering resentment on the part of the scribes and Pharisees. All we hear is that everyone was amazed and glorified God for the incredible things they had seen. Mark even says that "they were all astounded." Is it possible that this healing miracle had been so awe-inspiring as to convince even educated men who ought to have been outraged at Jesus' not-so-veiled claims of divinity? Or was there something compelling about the way he spoke, the way he looked at them? Whatever it was, on this day, those men seem to have gone away believing it was possible that this Jesus was something rather more than an ordinary man. He wasn't yet threatening their status or their worldview, wasn't yet demanding that they change in response to what they saw. So they listened to his preposterous claims, saw his impossible deeds, and wondered: Who is this man who makes all the world want to draw near?

Chapter Twelve

Reaching Out to the Broken

37. The Call of Matthew: *Matthew 9:9–13*; Mark 2:13–17; Luke 5:27–32

Jesus had collected quite a crowd of hangers-on at this point. Some he had called to follow him; others had invited themselves. But as far as we know, all those he had called thus far were "the right sort." They may have been simple and uneducated, mostly fishermen, but they were decent men. People may not have been particularly impressed by his choice of company, but at least they weren't outraged. Matthew changed all that.

After he left the scene where he had forgiven the sins of the paralytic, Jesus wanted to make a further point about his relationship with sinners. He also wanted to save Matthew's soul.

Matthew was a tax collector, the most hated sort of Jew. Tax collectors were traitors, collaborators (on par with Nazi collaborators in conquered nations) who worked with the Gentile oppressors to keep Israel subjugated. They collected the taxes demanded by Rome but were permitted to collect more besides to line their own pockets. And if treacherous
extortion wasn't bad enough, they worked so closely with Acts 10:28;
Gentiles that maintaining ritual purity would have been all 11:2–3

but impossible. In the eyes of most Jews, they were scum. Intimidating, powerful scum, but scum just the same.

When Jesus walked past Matthew, he ought to have ignored him, or possibly sneered. Instead, Jesus looked past the label and saw the person. He called, "Follow me."

It wasn't the first time the crowds had heard him say these words. For Peter, Andrew, James, John, and Philip, hearing
Mk 1:17; Jn 1:43 them again may have sent a thrill of memory through them, making them stand up straighter as they remembered having been chosen.

Until they realized who was being addressed this time. They had felt that there was something special about them, being the chosen few called to follow Jesus. But Matthew? This tax collector? There must be some mistake. Such a man could never be a follower of Jesus.

Yet Matthew — whose whole life up to that point had been about his own gain — immediately got up from his collection post and left everything behind. Not the way Peter
Lk 5:1–11 and the fishermen had, leaving an old boat and some moldy nets. Matthew left piles of cash. He simply walked away. Then he took what he had at home and spent it on a lavish banquet in Jesus' honor.

When a public sinner, a man essentially involved in organized crime, has a party, who comes? Other public sinners. The house was filled with them. And while we may be used to the idea that Jesus ate with prostitutes and tax collectors, this was actually the first time that he did. A major shift in his ministry was happening here: Having established his supernatural powers and teaching authority, he was ready to get to the heart of his mission — calling sinners to holiness.

But he didn't do it by standing on a street corner screaming accusations. He did it by loving them, by sitting down and listening to their stories and laughing with them. He broke bread with them in a culture where a shared meal symbolized a shared life.

This table fellowship was essential to Jesus' ministry. With it, he told sinners that he loved them, even as they were.

Nobody could mistake Jesus' preaching as condoning sin; it would have been much easier to misinterpret his words as a condemnation of sinners. But when he broke bread with them and entered into their lives, he told them that his love wasn't contingent on their behavior. When we love people in their sin, we give them the courage to fight for holiness because they know that they are not their sin. They are loved. Lk 17:2

And all of this began because of Matthew's past. Or, rather, his present — after all, it had only been a few hours since his conversion. Jesus took the ugliness of Matthew's sin, his status as an outcast, and used it for the sake of the Gospel. This is God's economy, in which nothing is wasted, not even our sin.

For Mark and Luke, Matthew's past as a tax collector was so shameful that they used another name for him: Levi (possibly his Hebrew name or his given name that he changed after his conversion). They didn't want to bring shame upon the esteemed apostle by making his past life known. Matthew, on the other hand, had no problem confessing it. His sins had been forgiven, and he was able to see how God's Providence had worked through his terrible choices to bring souls to Jesus who would never have come to dinner at the home of Peter or John. In fact, Matthew situates the story of his call in the middle of ten astonishing miracles in his eighth and ninth chapters. The message is clear: it was a miracle that Jesus called Matthew, that he wanted Matthew. It was a miracle that Matthew responded to that call. All those years later, Matthew was still stunned by it.

Of course, not everyone was delighted by Jesus' friendship with Matthew and the others. The scribes and Pharisees commented on it to his disciples, but Jesus was the one who responded: "Those who are well do not need a physician, but the sick do." Implicit in Jesus' statement here is that every one of us is a sinner, all of us in need of repentance, but these men who objected to his love of sinners didn't hear it that way. They heard only that Jesus was eager to surround himself with sinners — an odd choice, they thought, for a supposed Messiah.

Indignant though they must have felt to see this purportedly righteous man talking and laughing with sinners, his scriptural quotation surely bothered them more. "I desire
Hos 6:6
mercy, not sacrifice," he said, quoting the prophet Hosea. The scribes and Pharisees were meticulous in their observance of the law. They offered sacrifices and tithes and purified themselves assiduously. But — at least in this moment — they didn't rejoice when they saw sinners coming to God. If they weren't pleased at the conversion of sinners, over
Ez 18:23
whose repentance God delights, could their religious observance really be intended to please God? Many of us would do well to ask ourselves the same question.

38. Fasting with the Bridegroom: Matthew 9:14–17; Mark 2:18–22; *Luke 5:33–39*; John 3:27–30

Such words about sinners and sacrifice couldn't help but get people wondering about Jesus' orthodoxy. Now, suddenly, they began to realize: They had never seen Jesus fast, or his disciples either. So the disciples of John approached to ask a genuine question: Why don't your disciples fast?

They were probably expecting some simple answer — mercy is better than fasting, or the like. Instead, Jesus took this opportunity to speak a truth that he had only implied
Hos 2:21–22; Is 54:5; 62:4–5; Ez 16; Song of Songs
thus far: He was the bridegroom of Israel promised by the prophets.

"Can the wedding guests mourn as long as the bridegroom is with them?" he asked. Indeed, it might be merely a metaphor, but it was an odd one given the lack of an obvious bride in the scenario. Instead, he was reminding the Baptist's followers of what John himself had said of Jesus: "You yourselves can testify that I said [that] I am not the Messiah, but that I was sent before him. The one who has the bride is the bridegroom; the best man, who stands and listens to him, rejoices greatly at the bridegroom's voice. So this joy of mine has been made complete. He must increase; I must decrease."

When Jesus called himself the bridegroom, then, they

heard bridegroom-Messiah and echoes of Jeremiah's prom-
ised restoration of Jerusalem. They recalled that John, like Jer 33:11, 15
the best man in a Jewish wedding, had brought the people of
Israel to Jesus, a bride to her groom. John had felt no need to
compete with Jesus; he rejoiced that Jesus had come to take
his bride. The Baptist was happy to decrease before the true
bridegroom of God's people, the one who loved his people Rv 19:7; 21:9
with a complete, self-emptying, life-giving love.

John had called Jesus the bridegroom, and Jesus spoke here of the time of the bridegroom's departure, his wedding night, which would be an occasion of fasting for his guests. Later we'll see Jesus unite with his bride the Church on the marriage bed of the cross, an occasion of fasting and mourning that would bring great rejoicing. Here, though, his words meant little to those who heard them — they understood only that his followers would one day fast.

Even this, Jesus was careful to point out, wouldn't be
a mere return to the way they had fasted before. Jesus had
come to do something entirely new, and the framework of
the Old Covenant couldn't hold it. The New Covenant he
was establishing wouldn't be the law with some grace poured
over it, or the 613 old rules with a few extras. He was inviting
them to a complete renewal of humanity's relationship with
God, a new cloak rather than a patched one. Just as old wine- Jer 31:31–34
skins are brittle and easily burst, a heart that clings exclu-
sively to God's covenant with Moses will be unable to stretch
when invited into the New Covenant as it is filled with the
Holy Spirit. We have to be new wineskins, with hearts that
are offered to the Lord to be shaped however he wills.

39. The Compassion of Jesus and the Call of the Twelve: Matthew 9:35—10:4; *Mark 3:13–19*; Luke 6:12–16

At the beginning of Jesus' ministry, his followers had come and gone. There was no clear inner circle, nobody who had been given any sort of authority. But as the Lord traveled the countryside preaching and healing, it became more and

more clear that the work was too much for one man — even
the God-man. It was time for him to call a group of men
not just to follow but eventually to be sent out. The people's
needs touched the heart of their Redeemer, who could not
Mk 6:34; leave them as they were, "like sheep without a shepherd."
Nm 27:17 Jesus echoed the plea of Moses here, asking his followers to
pray for laborers for the harvest, then satisfied it by providing
the people of God with leaders to shepherd them.

Having asked the people to beg the Father for leaders, for diligent laborers in the vineyard and shepherds who
Jn 10:14–15 would lead the people in the model of the Good Shepherd,
Jesus went up the mountain to pray. He spent the whole
night in prayer, discerning who the Twelve would be and
holding them up before the throne of the Father; truly, the
Twelve were begotten in prayer.

It's interesting to note that there's no single theme that
unites Jesus' times of prayer. It stands to reason that he would
Lk 3:21; 5:16; pray before choosing his closest followers, but the Gospels also
9:18; Mt 14:23; speak of Jesus at prayer many other times: at his baptism; after
11:25–27; healing people; before asking the Twelve who they thought he
Lk 9:28–29; 11:1; was; before walking on water; after reproaching unrepentant
Jn 11:41–42; towns; during the Transfiguration; before teaching his disci-
17:1–26; ples to pray; before raising Lazarus; at the Last Supper; during
Lk 22:41–45; the agony in the Garden; and from the cross. Above all, the
23:34, 46; Gospels tell us, Jesus prayed. Not only when there was a deci-
Mt 27:46 sion to be made, not only when he needed strength, not only
when he was jubilant, not only when he had time. At all times,
in every mood, for every reason, Jesus prayed.

This time he spent the entire night in prayer. One wonders how often that happened, as the Son became so caught
up in love of the Father and the Spirit that the needs of his
body seemed unimportant. Here Jesus prayed about and for
the Twelve, begging that they be strengthened, just as he
Jn 17 would pray for them again the night before he died. The next
morning, he called them up into the mountains, as revolu-
2 Mc 5:27 tionaries gathered their followers. Whom did he call? "Those
whom he wanted." These were the ones he longed to be with,

the ones he looked forward to traveling with and laughing with and even correcting. We who have been baptized into this call often need to be reminded of the reason we were chosen: Jesus wanted us.

The Synoptics all name the Twelve, beginning with Peter (whom Jesus would appoint their leader) and ending with Mt 16:18–19
Judas, the betrayer. It's as though the Evangelists were reluctant even to speak his name, the man the apostles had once loved and now struggled daily to forgive.

In that group, there were men who would never have chosen to speak to one another. Matthew had been a Roman collaborator while Simon had been a Zealot, a member of the party most interested in violent revolution to overthrow Rome. These two had been sworn enemies, and now they were colleagues, friends, even brothers. Surely some of the Twelve must have been put off by Peter's brash ways or Nathanael's arrogance, and one or two may have found Judas something of a sycophant. But they had been called, and they would learn to love each other, not because they were Jn 13:34;
particularly loving but because Jesus had first loved them. 1 Jn 4:10

All told, there were twelve of them, as there were twelve tribes of Israel and twelve rulers over the kingdom under the great King Solomon. The King of Israel, the Son of David, 1 Kgs 4:7
the new Moses was calling forth a new Israel, initially composed of descendants of Abraham but soon to be opened to all nations. His Church wouldn't be a replacement of the kingdom of Israel, but a fulfillment. As Israel was "a kingdom of priests, a holy nation," so would the new Israel be, the Ex 19:6; 1 Pt 2:9
Twelve first and foremost.

Initially these men were called but not sent. Jesus invited them to follow him and asked them to stay close to him — both for their sake and for his. Then, as now, the job of Christians was above all to be with Jesus. They heard him preach and witnessed many miracles. They wrestled with things they did not understand. They heard him call their names, wept over all that was being asked of him, looked into his eyes and felt that he was worth all of it. For months, perhaps, they were simply called. Simply his. Being sent could wait.

40. Raising the Widow of Nain's Son: Luke 7:11–17

Jesus had now worked any number of healing miracles, to
the great astonishment of the crowds. But if there's one thing
1 Kgs 17:17–24; they knew for certain, it was that the dead stay dead. Elijah
2 Kgs 4:32–37; and Elisha may have raised a handful of people in the Old
13:21 Testament, but that was then. The people following Jesus
couldn't have imagined him to be stronger even than death. So when they arrived at Nain in his company and discovered that they had walked in on a funeral, surely even his disciples weren't expecting much.

It was the funeral of a young man, the only son of his widowed mother. This was more than just heartbreaking; it was devastating. With no husband or son to protect her and provide for her, she would likely be destitute before long. As Jesus saw her crying in the funeral procession, his heart
Jn 19:25; ached for her — and, perhaps, for his own Mother whose
Lk 2:35 heart would soon be pierced by the same sword.

"Do not weep," he said, an odd word of comfort to a grieving mother during her son's funeral. But Jesus wasn't chastising her for her grief, he was putting a stop to it. He walked over to the coffin, touched it, and said to the corpse, "Young man, I tell you, arise!"

The entire episode must have been shocking in its impropriety. He interrupted a funeral procession, told the mother of the deceased to stop crying, grabbed the coffin, and told a dead body to get up. The crowd would have been outraged — until they were astonished.

The dead man sat up and began to speak.

They had seen him die. He had been dead for days. They had mourned over his body. Such men do not rise.

But this one did.

And while they had heard stories of resurrections worked centuries before by the great prophets of old, even Elijah and Elisha had raised the dead only through dramatically, physically beseeching the Lord, stretching their bodies over top of the corpses they raised while begging God (loudly in Elijah's case) to restore life. Jesus merely spoke a word, with a nonchalance that betrayed his familiarity with giving life.

Then, it seems, he helped the man up, took him to his mother, and moved quietly out of the crowd while everyone was busy exclaiming over what they had seen. There's no story of what they said to him or how they looked at him after he had exhibited such power. But while they praised God, they were afraid. It's one thing to pray for a miracle. It's another to know a man who can raise the dead. We ought to feel some of that same awe in the face of a God as powerful as ours.

"A great prophet has arisen," they cried out, and "God
has visited his people." It was truer than they realized, even
those who thought he might be the "prophet" like Moses Dt 18:15
who had been foretold. They saw only the power of God
working through his servant, but Emmanuel, God-with-us,
had indeed visited his people. He had pitched his tabernacle
among them, and they would see greater things than they Jn 1:14
had ever imagined in the years — and centuries — to come.

41. Jairus's Daughter and the Hemorrhaging Woman: Matthew 9:18–26; *Mark 5:21–43*; Luke 8:40–56

This wonder and awe reached from the desperately poor to
the shockingly wealthy, touching even the religious leaders of
the Jews. Joseph of Arimathea was a member of the Sanhedrin (the council of leaders of the Jews) and a Christ-follower
so committed that he asked for Jesus' body after Jesus had
been executed. Nicodemus, too, served on the Sanhedrin Jn 19:38
and (though it took him some time to commit) ultimately Jn 3:1–15; 7:50–
declared himself for Jesus. Many less prominent men were 52; 19:39–40
also open to hearing the Good News and even bowing before
Jesus.

When Jairus, a synagogue official, approached Jesus, that's just what he did: He fell at Jesus' feet. Jesus had just arrived in town, having crossed the sea "in the boat" (a detail

Mark specifies that would be implied for any other man). From the moment Jesus disembarked, he was surrounded by a crowd, but Jairus was desperate. His only daughter, a little girl of twelve, was dying. He pushed through the crowd and begged on his knees, "Please, come lay your hands on her."

Without a word, Jesus followed. The crowd was pressing in on them and it was difficult to move through the throng of people who had come to see Jesus. Some were seeking miracles of their own, others looking for God. Some were there to witness a spectacle, while others were sure they'd find a fraud. But in among the seekers and the scoffers was a broken, wretched woman. She had been bleeding for twelve years, the very length of the life of Jairus's little girl. And while Jairus hoped for the preservation of this child of twelve, the hemorrhaging woman longed for redemption of her twelve years of suffering.

The problem wasn't just the pain or the constant exhaustion brought on by the resulting anemia. The problem was isolation. When a woman was menstruating, the law
Lv 15:19–27 declared her unclean. For one week out of a month, with all the women cycling together, this might have come as a welcome relief from the incessant demands of life. But this woman had been unclean for twelve years. She couldn't be touched. A chair she sat in would be unclean as well. She wouldn't have been invited to another person's home, nor would they be inclined to visit her. She could never worship in the Temple.

And having visited one doctor after another, she had spent all she had. She was sick and exhausted and poor and alone.

Then she heard tell of a wonder-worker, a man who made the lame walk and raised the dead. A flicker of hope grew within her: Maybe this man could heal her, could restore her to her community.

But how to approach him? He was always surrounded by crowds, and she, being unclean, couldn't push through a crowd. The people who knew her would be horrified that she had made them all unclean. And when she got to him, what then? Could she speak of this flow of blood to a strange man before everybody? She couldn't. It would never work.

Through her discouragement, though, a voice spoke: *If you just touch him, that will be enough.* So she covered her face and left the darkness and isolation of her home. She moved into the crowd, ignoring her certainty that she wasn't worthy to be there. Still hiding in her shame, she pursued Jesus, reached out, and touched his cloak.

Immediately the flow of blood dried up. Her body had been healed, in such dramatic fashion that she felt it even in the moment. But Jesus wasn't done with her yet. It wasn't enough for her to be healed of her affliction if she still lived in the darkness of shame. He had to call her out, to invite her into the light and heal her wounded soul as well. Ps 139:11–12; 1 Pt 2:9

So he stopped walking and turned around. The woman was likely moving away through the crowd, overjoyed but still afraid. When she heard him ask, "Who touched me?" she must have been terrified. She had been healed, but at what cost? What would he say to a woman who had defiled him, who had stolen his blessing? What would she say to the crowd that would surely be out for blood when they knew what she had done to them all? Gn 27

The disciples, meanwhile, had no idea what was going on. Jesus was asking an unreasonable question. Who had touched him? Dozens, perhaps hundreds of people. He was surrounded — what could he mean by asking who touched him? It was nonsensical.

Jesus wasn't asking them, though. Nor was he particularly concerned with their response. He had eyes only for a woman who had been cured in body but still had great need of healing.

With immense courage, she walked back toward him, trembling in her fear. She fell down at his feet and explained the whole story: her suffering, her faith, even how she had compromised all those around her by pushing past them while unclean. And then she cringed, waiting to be reprimanded.

No blows came, nor shouts, nor angry mutterings. The crowd waited in silence. Only Jesus spoke. "Daughter," he said. Again, a moment of intimacy while surrounded by a crowd. Jesus was clearly uninterested in her unclean status — he purified the unclean by his very presence. Instead, he was pleased that she had had such faith, not only to believe that he could heal her but also to trust him enough that she returned to tell her story. He called to her not in order to learn what had happened but because he wanted to know her, wanted to look into her eyes and let her look into his. He wanted to set her free emotionally and spiritually as well as physically.

This moment of encounter was essential, as the woman brought her shame into the light and had it transformed by
Jn 8:12 the Lord. When Jesus spoke, he told her, "Go in peace and be cured of your affliction." This imperative is significant. The woman had already been cured of her illness, but Jesus offered healing of her isolation and her shame as well. *Go,* he said, *and live in the freedom that you've been given.*

Like the bystanders, we've been so caught up in the drama and the beauty of this story that we may have forgotten it's an interruption. Jesus was on his way to save a little girl from death, but he stopped. He didn't see the hemorrhaging woman as a distraction; she, too, was a daughter.

In all three Synoptic Gospels, Jesus calls the woman "daughter"; it's the only time he ever addresses a woman this way. Certainly, he was speaking to her, telling her how deeply she was loved, promising her that even in her twelve long years of loneliness she had never been forsaken. But he was also speaking to Jairus. Through this whole episode Jairus has said nothing, but one has to imagine that he was beyond impatient. His daughter was dying, and this alleged miracle-worker was chatting with the crowd about people being in his personal space? And when the culprit came forward, it was clear that she was nobody special — just a beggar whose long years of isolation must have made her so desperate to be seen and heard that when she told Jesus "the whole truth," it couldn't have been a short story. Jairus was respectful enough not to hurry the Master along, but he must have been panicking, even raging within himself.

So when Jesus called the woman "Daughter," he was speaking to her, but he was also reminding Jairus: *Your daughter is ill. I know how hard that is. I understand. But this woman is also somebody's daughter. This woman is also somebody. She deserves to be healed just as much as your daughter does.* Perhaps in that moment Jairus learned what we so often need to be reminded of: how to see each person not as an object or an obstacle but as the beloved of God.

In that moment, he heard the voice of a friend telling him, "Your daughter is dead; do not trouble the teacher any longer." Has such heartbreaking news ever been delivered in a more callous way? The one speaking seems most concerned with getting Jairus away from Jesus, either because it was unseemly for a synagogue official to seek help from such a one as Jesus, or because Jesus was respected and busy and his time wasn't to be wasted. Either way, the one delivering the message clearly didn't know Jesus, didn't know what he was capable of and didn't know his heart — that he would never abandon a man whose daughter had just died, whether or not he planned to raise her.

Mercifully, Jesus responded before Jairus could. "Do not be afraid," he said to a man whose greatest fear had just come to pass, "just have faith." He hurried Jairus through the streets, accompanied by an ever-growing crowd, until they arrived at a house filled with wailing people. Jesus took his three closest friends — Peter, James, and John — and pushed past the loudly weeping mourners, asking, "Why this commotion and weeping? The child is not dead but asleep."

At that, they ridiculed him, bitterly assuring Jesus that they knew well what death looked like, and this girl was dead. Like us, they refused to believe Jesus' promises, laughing at him with scorn and with the cynicism born of a broken heart. But Jesus wasn't concerned about their unbelief.

He shooed them out of the house — surely offending many — and went to the room with the beautiful young corpse inside.

Once again, he recited no incantations, nor did he lie on
1 Kgs 17:17–24; 2 top of the body like Elijah and Elisha had. He simply took
Kgs 4:32–37 the little girl by the hand and said to her, "Little girl, I say to you, arise!" It's telling that Mark uses the Aramaic here, a sign that his source (Peter) had been so struck by those words that he remembered them exactly — their inflection, the tone of Jesus' voice, all of it. He must have spoken with great power and great tenderness, as her parents looked on.

And she rose. Her father sobbed and her mother gasped, and both held her close and then looked into her eyes and laughed while crying. The child wasn't just resuscitated, having been comatose and now conscious again. She got up and walked around, as though nothing had ever been wrong with her.

Jesus, ever practical, told her nearly hysterical parents to give her some food, with a nonchalance that must have astounded his disciples almost as much as her resurrection had. Jesus had a purpose in bringing Peter, James, and John with him. These three disciples watched him raise the dead and
Lk 9:28–36 would later see him glorified on Mount Tabor so that when
Mt 26:36–46 he prayed at Gethsemane and climbed up Calvary, they would remember his power over death and have hope. Only John, it seems, took this lesson to heart, returning to Jesus'
Jn 19:26–27 side after he had slept and fled from Gethsemane. But later, when they began to hear whisperings of his empty tomb, Peter and James must have remembered. They must have thought back to that empty bedroom, so recently a tomb. And over all the years they spent working and preaching and longing for him, they must have hoped to hear the same words Jairus's daughter heard: *Arise, Peter. Arise, John. Arise,*
Lk 15:18 *James. Let us rise and go to our Father.* Made well like Jairus's daughter. Made whole like the hemorrhaging woman. Be-
Rv 21:5 cause Jesus makes all things new.

Chapter Thirteen

An Unpredictable Messiah

42. Messengers from John the Baptist: Matthew 11:2–6; *Luke 7:18–23*

This run of miracles totals ten in a row in Matthew's Gospel
(with the less obvious miracle of his own call and response
toward the middle, surrounded by equally astonishing feats). Mt 9:9–13
This is Jesus the new Moses performing ten miracles of healing and peace and restoration, just as Moses of old had called
down ten plagues of devastation by the power of God. Jesus' Ex 7—11
power was becoming increasingly evident. But as Jesus was
increasing in the eyes of the people, John the Baptist was lan- Jn 3:30
guishing in prison, having run afoul of Herod Antipas, the
son of that Herod who had ordered the slaughter of the in- Mt 2:15–18
nocents in Bethlehem. Both Matthew and Luke tell of John's
arrest at the very beginning of Jesus' ministry, sent to prison Mt 4:12;
for his own ministry as forerunner of the Messiah. While he Lk 3:19–20
waited and wondered just what might come next, John sent
his disciples to Jesus, as he had sent Andrew and John earli- Jn 1:35–37
er. This time, though, they had a specific question they had
been sent to ask: "Are you the one who is to come, or should
we look for another?"

This question can be read in a number of ways. Maybe John was second-guessing himself and sent his disciples to determine if Jesus really was the one sent by God. Maybe he was frustrated with his captivity and was asking to be set free, something like, *Are you the Messiah or not? Because if so, I'd like you to do something about my imprisonment.*

But John the Baptist wasn't an uncertain or angry type. He spoke with clarity, fully aware of what the consequences of his words might be. Impassioned he may have been, but never impetuous. No, this mission he sent his disciples on seems to have been more pedagogical than anything: *You're seeking the Messiah. I've told you that's not my role. Go see Jesus and ask him if he is the Messiah.* Or perhaps, *You keep asking me why Jesus hasn't set me free if he's the Messiah. But no matter*
Jn 1:19–28 *how often I tell you it's his call to make, you won't listen. Why don't you go ask him instead?*

Still, he may have felt a sliver of hope that this reminder of his plight would encourage Jesus to set his cousin free.
Is 61:1; Ps 146:7; After all, they had been told that the Messiah would come
Lk 4:18 to proclaim liberty to captives and release to prisoners. John demanded nothing, but perhaps he hoped.

Jesus' heart must have ached, knowing what John suffered and what he was about to suffer. But the prophet who had gone before him in life would go before him in death as well. This liberation was not to be his — not in this life, anyway.

In a characteristic response, Jesus didn't directly answer their question. He didn't say, "Yes, I am the Messiah"; instead, he showed them. He healed the sick and the blind, he cast out demons, and then he told them just what he had done, just what it was promised that the Messiah would do: "The blind regain their sight, the lame walk, lepers are cleansed, the deaf hear, the dead are raised, and the poor have the good news proclaimed to them" — all things Jesus had done. This catalogue of miracles is a reference to several Old Testament
Ps 146:7; Is prophecies about the Messiah, but with a notable absence: Un-
35:5–6; 61:1 like Isaiah and the psalmist — unlike Jesus himself at the be-
Lk 4:18 ginning of his public ministry — this time Jesus said nothing about setting prisoners free.

"Are you the one who is to come?" they asked. *Yes,* he said, *I am, even if you don't see the kingdom of God coming in the way you expected.* "And blessed is the one who takes no offense at me." *Blessed are you, John, for accepting that I could set you free but I'm not going to. Blessed are those who will not be scandalized by my death on the cross. Blessed are those who spend years praying for one thing and still follow me when I tell them no. Blessed are those who accept what I teach through my Church even when they don't like it. Blessed are those who spend their lives in captivity to fear or persecution or addiction and still glorify God.*

It may not have been the answer John wanted; anyone would hope for freedom, hope to live. But when the cousin he loved, the Messiah he foretold, the God he served gave him such an answer, *I will not set you free, but I will bless you in your suffering*, the forerunner joined his kinswoman in offering his fiat to the Lord. He didn't need God to conform to Lk 1:38
his expectations; he was happy to let God be God.

43. Testimony to John the Baptist: Matthew 11:7–19; 17:10–13; Mark 9:11–13; *Luke 7:24–35*

As John's followers walked away, returning to their master with a message that was an odd mixture of joy and sorrow, Jesus began to speak of his cousin and the work John had done. There's pain underlying his words, knowing as he did that John would soon die for his refusal to vacillate. But while the Baptist had fearlessly proclaimed the truth, Jesus knew that so many who had gone out to see him had done so just for the curiosity of it.

In this moment, Jesus questioned their motives in following John. *Were you looking for someone who would bend to your desires? A reed swayed by any wind, a weak man who would affirm your inclinations? No? Then maybe you were looking for a king, a man caught up in his own dignity who wears fine clothes dyed with the blood of his people? No? Then why are you here?* Jesus was exposing their small-mindedness, these people who went to hear a prophet speak and yet objected because he spoke like a prophet. The same people wanted Jesus to heal but never to challenge.

Interestingly, he set John up in opposition to Herod here. Herod dressed in rich clothes and lived in a palace; Herod also had a coin struck with the image of a reed on it. But where Herod was weak and capricious, delighting in vice, John would not be moved. He decried sin and proclaimed the kingdom of God, while the false king of the Jews reveled in his palace.

It's as though Jesus was saying to his listeners, *These are your choices. Either you stand with John in the way of righteousness and suffer the consequences, or you sell your soul like Herod. But if you choose John, know this: John is a prophet and more than a prophet. He is the one sent to announce the coming of the Messiah. He is the greatest man born in the Old Covenant, greater even than Moses. But even John is nothing compared to those who will be washed in my blood.*

Lest they misunderstand, Jesus spoke once more about
John's tremendous importance: He was the messenger sent
by God to prepare the way for the Messiah, the one foretold
Mal 3:1 by Malachi in some of the last words spoken to God's people
before the prophets fell silent. Malachi went on to clarify
that this coming prophet who would prepare the way of the
Mal 3:23–24 Lord would come in the spirit of Elijah, playing the same
role as that great prophet of old. "He is Elijah," Jesus stated
simply. After John's death, Jesus would explain this to his
apostles once more, telling them that John had gone before
him preparing the way in the spirit of Elijah.

With John's impending death looming large in his mind, Jesus wasn't content to leave the people in their complacency, their insistence on criticizing both sides while remaining in the mediocre middle. Like all of us, the people of Jesus' time had certain expectations of how God ought to act and what a holy man ought to look like — he should not eat too many meals or too many locusts. Though John was clearly a prophet, they would have preferred a gentler message. Though Jesus worked wonders, he was too much of a libertine for them.

They passed judgment on the Messiah and his prophet because they didn't like their styles.

The words Jesus placed on their lips are worth remarking on. He accused them of calling him "a glutton and a drunkard" — the same language used to disown an unruly son in the Mosaic law and then have him stoned. Though their allegations against Jesus were still nothing too scandalous (*he eats with sinners and doesn't fast*), Jesus knew where their criticisms would soon lead, escalating until his enemies demanded the death of the Son for not conforming to their expectations.

Dt 21:18–21

44. The Anointing by the Sinful Woman: Luke 7:36–50

Immediately after this rebuke of those who objected to Jesus' love of sinners, Luke tells the story of a sinful woman whose behavior toward Jesus scandalized everybody. Jesus had been invited to dine at the home of a Pharisee named Simon. It seems this wasn't a friendly invitation, as Simon extended no courtesies to Jesus. He didn't greet him with a kiss or even give him water with which to wash. Jesus was there to be interrogated and corrected, not befriended.

As Jesus reclined at table, a woman who was a public sinner approached him. It's worth questioning why a woman who was known to be a sinner had free access to Simon the Pharisee's house. What relationship existed between her and Simon that allowed her to enter his home unchallenged? Perhaps the presence of such a guest meant Simon's doors were open that day to any who sought to hear the teacher speak — or perhaps there's more hypocrisy in Simon than at first seems evident.

In any event, when she heard that Jesus was with Simon, the woman knew that he would not be well-treated. She rushed to Simon's house and slipped into the room where they were preparing to eat. She watched the disdain with which Simon and his friends treated Jesus, this man who looked at sinners as though they were human beings deserving of love, and she began to weep. How could they act as though he were beneath them? He who treated lepers and centurions with the same degree of kindness, the same disarming love. She couldn't make them treat him with courtesy, but she could do something. She could treat him as he deserved, not merely as a guest but as the king he was.

So this disdained and derided woman brought out an alabaster flask of ointment. As Jesus reclined at table, she moved up behind him and began to wash his feet with her tears. If we recall that only a slave could be asked to remove
Jn 1:27 his master's sandals, we begin to see the woman's willingness to be debased. Moreover, a woman typically washed the feet of her husband alone. The same section of the Talmud (Ketuvot 96a) that says that only slaves removed their master's sandals (unlike disciples, who served their masters in all other ways) also tells us that women were never expected to wash the feet of their husbands' relatives but only of their husbands. Thus we see what an act of intimacy this is.

As the woman bathed Jesus' feet with her tears, wiped them with her hair, and kissed them, the other men in the room must have been appalled. That Jesus would let a woman touch him in this way was scandalous enough, but *such* a woman! The atmosphere in the room must have been tense, even hostile. But for Jesus and the sinful woman, nobody else mattered. She had uncovered her hair before him, a bridal act in a society where women typically kept their heads covered. In this moment, she was laying down her past and giving herself over completely to him. And he, for his part, was accepting it. The tears that accompanied this act of intimacy make it clear that this is no attempt at seduction on the part of the woman, but an act of love and gratitude by one who had been forgiven much.

However tender the moment, though, at a certain point Jesus had to return his attention to his host, who had watched this exchange with disgust. If Jesus were truly a prophet, Simon sneered, he would have known of this woman's sin and (it's implied) kept his distance. Jesus didn't need to read minds to know what Simon was thinking; surely the expression on Simon's face spoke volumes. Unwilling to leave Simon in his sin of arrogance and self-righteousness, Jesus offered a very simple parable, albeit one whose relevance the Pharisee had trouble seeing. Two men are forgiven debts, one debt large, the other small. Which man will love his benefactor more?

Simon's answer seems almost sullen: "The one, I suppose, whose larger debt was forgiven." One can imagine him following it with a petulant, *Obviously*. Jesus had entered his home but not his heart.

"You have judged rightly," Jesus responded, but before Simon had time to congratulate himself (or to roll his eyes at the simplicity of the question), Jesus continued. "Do you see this woman?"

It wasn't merely a rhetorical question, a means of gesturing to her. Jesus was genuinely asking: *Do you see her? Or do you only see her sin? Can you look past her reputation and her actions and see a human being, created, willed, and loved by God?*

After Simon had reluctantly turned his attention to this woman whom he viewed as beneath his notice, Jesus began to compare the two of them. Surely, this was what Simon had been doing all along: He was righteous, she was sinful; he was respected, she was disdained. But Simon didn't come out so well in Jesus' estimation. *You invited me to your home, but didn't even give me water to wash with, contrary to all rules of hospitality. But she was so concerned with honoring me that when she saw you wouldn't provide water, she bathed my feet with her tears. You offered no towel, but she dried my feet with her hair. Such love, and at such cost! You didn't greet me with a kiss, but she has poured kisses upon me. You didn't anoint my head, but she brought costly ointment to anoint me.*

If Simon had any shame at all, this litany must have left him cringing; even an adversary deserved to be treated with respect when a guest in one's home. The woman's generosity was a reproach to him, but Jesus had more to say: "Her many sins have been forgiven; hence, she has shown great love." The word *hence* is tremendously significant here. She was not forgiven much because she had loved; she loved because she had been forgiven. She had done great evil, but God's mercy had washed her clean. Because of her gratitude, she now loved Jesus far more.

Perhaps we've become accustomed to the astonishing
ways of Providence, forgetting what a miracle it is that God
Rom 8:28 continually works even the ugliest of things for good. Though
he doesn't desire sin, he is able to take our sin and use even that
for his glory so that "where sin increased, grace overflowed all
Rom 5:20 the more." What a gift to know that our most heartbreaking
choices, our vilest sins have become an avenue for God's grace.
If we surrender to his mercy, he can make even the ugliest of
backstories into glorious hagiography.

It's only after teaching Simon this lesson that Jesus assured the woman that she had truly been forgiven. All that she'd done, all that she'd risked, had been in the hope that she might be forgiven. When she'd entered Simon's house, she had known that Jesus might spit in her face and throw her out on the street. She'd heard tell of his mercy, maybe even caught a glimpse of his kind eyes, but her audacious act of love was shot through with uncertainty. She was still in her sin, and he had every right to treat her as Simon did. But somehow she knew that he would love her, even in her sin. Perhaps the reason we don't lay ourselves bare before the Lord is because we don't know him enough to trust him. The sinful woman — the forgiven woman — trusted first. She took the risk of opening herself up to the Lord when she didn't yet know him, and in so doing she gave hope to centuries of sinners, that they too might love much because of how much they've been forgiven.

Mk 2:7 Again, the bystanders scoffed at his claim to forgive sins,
but this time Jesus made no reply. In this moment, he wasn't
making a theological point. He was offering freedom to a
beloved daughter of God. "Your faith has saved you," he said,
Lk 8:48 as he did to the hemorrhaging woman, as he would soon

say to blind Bartimaeus and to the Samaritan leper. With this woman, there was no physical healing, only spiritual. In those other encounters, the physical healing was wrought as a means to the spiritual. Their faith brought them to Jesus, and that encounter brought healing and forgiveness and the promise of eternity. Mk 10:52; Lk 17:19

45. Women Following Jesus: Luke 8:1–3

Jesus' travels continued, in company with the Twelve and a group of women. The women's presence alone would have been shocking, but some of these women had formerly been possessed by demons. It's important to note how frequently Jesus flouted conventions, if only to remind ourselves that everything he did was deliberate. It's become popular to discount certain choices made by the Son of God as though he were a product of his times. A man who chose to travel with women who were seen as cursed or evil certainly felt free to make his own decisions, and nothing he said or did can be discounted as culturally conditioned. His followers understood this well, raising up women as leaders and evangelists in the early Church in imitation of the Master. Rom 16:1-7; Acts 16:14-15; Col 4:15; 2 Jn 1:1

This is also our first introduction to Mary Magdalene, a woman out of whom Jesus had cast seven demons, the woman to whom he would first appear after his resurrection. Jn 20:11–18 Mary Magdalene has been the subject of speculation at least since the Gospels were put to parchment, but the essentials are certain: She was deeply loved by Jesus. Her past did not determine her future in his kingdom, nor her ability to serve him in that moment. She who would become the Apostle to the Apostles wanted nothing more than to be with Jesus. All of these women — even more than their male counterparts — were willing to risk their reputations and their futures just to be with Jesus, just to hear him speak, to watch his look of compassion when he met the lonely and the suffering, to snatch a moment of conversation with him. If his promises didn't pan out, most of them would have nothing waiting for them when they slunk home in shame. He was worth the risk.

Among the other women who traveled with Jesus and his disciples was Joanna, the wife of Herod's steward, and thus a distinguished personage. She and others provided for Jesus and his entourage out of their generosity, and Jesus allowed himself to be served. He condescended not only to become a human being, but also to be beholden to human beings. He knew what it was to be needy, even to be a burden at times. When he entered into the human experience, he embraced all of it, even the moments of discomfort that we would gladly avoid. For us, he avoided none of it. And he avoided none of us, breaking down barriers and lavishing love with every step, every glance, every word. What would our world look like if we who claim to follow him chose also to love so recklessly?

Chapter Fourteen

Early Controversies

46. Sabbath Disputes: Matthew 12:1–21; Mark 2:23—3:6; *Luke 6:1–11; 13:10–17; 14:1–6*

Though he didn't stir up trouble unnecessarily, Jesus wasn't one to shy away from controversy; in fact, he often initiated it. Nowhere is this more obvious than in his constant provocation of debates about the Sabbath. It began simply enough, with the disciples snacking on grain as they walked through a field on the Sabbath. It might seem excessive for the Pharisees to have jumped on something so small, but Sabbath rest was more than just a legalistic observance. The Sabbath, observed every seventh day, was a sign of God's covenant with mankind. To keep the Sabbath was an act of worship of God; to break the Sabbath was akin to idolatry. In fact, Israel's disregard of the Sabbath was one of the covenant violations that had brought about the Babylonian Captivity in the sixth century BC. In a time when the Messiah was expected any day, it's no wonder the Pharisees were concerned about apparent violations of the Sabbath. They were trying to protect their nation.

Gn 2:3; Ex 20:8–11; 32:12–14

Jer 17:19–27; Neh 13:17–18

But their observance of the Sabbath had become something of an idol. The day was no longer a mini jubilee set aside for rest and worship; instead, it was a day of bondage to exacting constraints that often made it impossible for people to do good for one another. Moreover, the restrictions placed on the Sabbath weighed more heavily on the poor, who didn't have the means to make loopholes in Sabbath regulations that the rich did. Jesus' repeated violations of the Pharisees' understanding of the Sabbath (never of Scripture's actual requirements) do more than reframe our religious practices; they serve to explain the purpose of the Sabbath and, ultimately, of the human relationship with God as one that isn't about earning but about receiving.

When challenged about the grain his disciples were picking, Jesus referenced an incident in the life of King David, when David's followers were exempt from a divine regulation
1 Sm 21:2–7 because of the mission they were carrying out. "Have you not read what David did?" Jesus asked, a subtle insult levied against these men who defined themselves by their religious literacy.

The priests also worked in the Temple each Sabbath without violating the law, Jesus pointed out. Just so, Jesus' followers were serving him, and, Jesus said, "something greater than the temple is here." This claim alone would have merited a cry against blasphemy. What could be greater than the Temple, the center of the earth and locus of God's presence? But Jesus casually set himself up not only as the new
Jn 2:21 Temple but also as *greater* than the Temple. Greater than the Sabbath as well, it seems, for as Son of Man he was Lord of the Sabbath.

Jesus explained the heart of his understanding of the Sabbath here: "The sabbath was made for man, not man for the sabbath." Jesus never objected to religion or to ritual, he objected to empty ritual or religion that makes rules more important than a relationship with God and neighbor. All the rules and rituals of the Old Covenant existed to bring people into right relationship with the Lord and with one another, as do the rules and rituals prescribed by the New Covenant. It's only when the rules become the heart of religion, rather than an avenue to God's heart, that they become problematic.

Many of the Sabbath controversies are the result of Jesus' choice to heal on the Sabbath. Given that every recorded healing that he initiated took place on the Sabbath, it's clear that this was no coincidence. Jesus wanted his opponents to see that the Sabbath is an invitation to rest and rejoice in the Father, not to be bound by restrictions that keep people from acts of mercy.

Jn 5:1–18; 9:1–41

On one particular Saturday, Jesus began his Sabbath healing by calling to a man with a withered hand. The Pharisees had seen the man there and watched him, wondering not if Jesus *could* heal him — that seems to have been a given — but if he would. They knew that Jesus was shifting people's understanding of the Sabbath, so they waited to catch him.

Throughout this encounter, the Pharisees' attitude serves to prove Jesus' point. They saw a man who was suffering on the Sabbath and did nothing to help him; instead, they spent the holy day plotting to do evil. Jesus, meanwhile, called the man to him. Knowing that the Pharisees were watching, he addressed them directly: "Is it lawful to do good on the Sabbath? To save life rather than to destroy it?" There seems to be a reference here to the wars of the Maccabees. Two centuries earlier, the Jewish people had fought against the Greeks who ruled over them. Out of obedience to the law, they had refused to fight on the Sabbath — and were promptly slaughtered. Having determined that God was not glorified by their defeat, the Maccabees and their followers decided that they would defend themselves even on the Sabbath. Here, Jesus invoked that memory, when the Pharisees' ancestors had determined that it was just to take lives on the Sabbath, and asked how much more one ought to save lives.

1 Mc 2:31–41

Though they must have known what he was driving at with this question, pride hardened their hearts, and they refused to answer. Jesus was angry at their inability to see beyond their own convictions and grieved that their hearts felt no compassion for the suffering man. With a sigh of resignation, he turned to the man and healed him.

This was enough to seal Jesus' fate, even this early in his ministry. "The Pharisees went out and immediately took counsel with the Herodians against him to put him to death," Mark tells us — only three chapters into his Gospel! These two groups were sworn enemies, but both saw Jesus as a threat. Some of the Pharisees may genuinely have been concerned that Jesus' cavalier attitude toward the law would lead Israel further into sin. Others were clearly more concerned about preserving their own power and prestige. The Herodians, supporters of King Herod, were surely glad to rid themselves of any Messianic character who could so easily oust the non-Davidic (and non-Jewish) king whom they served. And so the self-appointed protectors of the Sabbath spent the Lord's day plotting with their enemies to kill the Lord's anointed.

Matthew tells of Jesus' response to the heartbreaking
(but unsurprising) news that these men for whom he was
preparing to lay down his life were preparing in turn to take
his life: He withdrew. But though he withdrew from that
place, he didn't withdraw from his people. He went right
back out to do the healing for which he'd come. In the face of
rejection, he continued to pour himself out. Matthew quotes
Isaiah: "Behold, my servant whom I have chosen, / my beloved in whom I delight; / I shall place my spirit upon him,
Is 42:1 / and he will proclaim justice to the Gentiles." These words
refer to our gentle Savior, who wouldn't break a bruised reed
Is 42:3 or quench a smoldering wick. This passage isn't merely praise
of Jesus' meek and mild nature, but a reminder of just who
he is: the beloved in whom the Father delights, on whom the
Spirit rests. We who may be taken aback by Jesus' seemingly
dismissive attitude toward the Sabbath are reminded of his
baptism, where the Father called Jesus beloved, insisting that
he was pleased with his Son, and where the Spirit came to
Mt 3:16–17 rest on Jesus. It's as though Matthew is reassuring us: *I know
this is a lot to take in. But remember who's speaking. This is the
one God has sent.* The same language would be used a few
chapters later, at the Transfiguration, when we see Jesus as

superior even to Moses and Elijah, with the Father further emphasizing his authority, saying, "Listen to him." Lk 9:28–36

There's something beautiful about this appeal to authority. Matthew acknowledges that what Jesus does and says might be confusing. Even those who knew him best were often baffled by his choices. But when we wonder and re- Jn 4:27
search and wrestle and still find ourselves unable to understand what the Lord is speaking to us or asking of us, this is our next step: to remember who he is. He is the beloved of the Father. He is the way, the truth, and the life. He is for us. Jn 14:6
All his words are true, and all his promises are trustworthy. And if we believe all that, following doesn't seem quite so difficult.

This conviction of Jesus' identity is the foundation we stand on as we see similar scenes of Sabbath healings (and their resultant controversy) played out throughout his public ministry. Luke tells of a woman who had been crippled for eighteen years by an evil spirit, bent double by her affliction. Jesus, it seems, interrupted his teaching to call out a healing from across the room. She hadn't asked for anything, but he saw the opportunity to offer her liberation and to remind his opponents that the Sabbath was an occasion for freedom, not bondage.

The healed woman stood up straight, the casual words of Jesus having cast out the spirit that had crippled her, and gave glory to God. But the leader of the synagogue responded like a seasoned bureaucrat. Rather than even pausing a moment to be impressed that this woman had been healed — a woman he had watched suffer for nearly twenty years — he was merely annoyed that protocol hadn't been followed. "There are six days when work should be done. Come on those days to be cured!" he barked.

It may appear that Jesus' patience had worn thin, but his response is exactly what the souls present that day needed to hear: "Hypocrites!" he cries out. "Ought she not to have been set free on the sabbath day?" He knew that her affliction had raged for eighteen years. Ever rational, he compared her bondage to that of livestock. Everyone unbinds his ox on the Sabbath; why not unbind this woman? His logic was so clear that his adversaries had nothing to say. Indeed, this time they were humiliated. It was clear that the rules they loved so much had become their god, at least in this respect.

Shortly thereafter, Luke tells of another healing, this time of a man with dropsy. Again, he asked his interlocutors, "Is it lawful to cure on the sabbath?" They had heard his arguments. They knew his reasoning was flawless. They knew his healings were supernatural, so it was clear God must have approved of the man's words. And yet they were unable to answer his question; their pride made it impossible for them to capitulate while their intelligence made it unthinkable for them to keep arguing.

47. The Healing of the Paralytic in Jerusalem: John 5:1–18

Twice more, Jesus healed on the Sabbath (though the last instance, found in John 9, we'll deal with in the next volume). In John's Gospel, we're told of several visits Jesus made to Jerusalem. During one of them, he first visited the pool of Bethesda. The people there believed that an angel came occasionally to stir the waters of the pool; after that happened, the first person to enter the pool would receive healing. Because of this tradition, there were many people there with various ailments and disabilities. Yet somehow (as far as we know), Jesus spoke only to one, offered healing only to one.

Scripture doesn't tell us why, though we can speculate. Whatever the specific reason was here, it likely remained unknown to the many people who weren't offered healing that day. And yet we know that Jesus loved them, too. He wanted their good. We must assume that somehow healing — or, at least, healing at that time — wasn't in their best interest. We have to trust, both with their pain as well as with our own unanswered prayers, that the God who loved us enough to
Rom 8:32 die for us will give us what we need, even if that means refusing to give us what we want.

The man approached by Jesus had been sick for thirty-eight years. That alone ought to warrant our compassion. But when Jesus approached him, he asked a question that strikes us as odd: "Do you want to be well?"

Of course he wanted to be well. Who would want to be sick? Especially after nearly forty years of suffering?

And yet it's a valid question. On a practical level, it's possible that the man knew how to do nothing but beg after so many years with a disability. Jesus didn't want to rob him of that income without his permission.

On a deeper level, he asked that man the same question he asks us when we come to him with our sin and fear and brokenness: Do you truly want to be well? Do you want to forgive? Do you want to do the hard work it will take to heal? Sometimes we ask for things in prayer that we don't truly want. Here, God, in his mercy, asked the man to think long and hard before asking again for his miracle.

Perhaps, in our lives, this question is more of an invitation from the Lord: Are you ready to be healed? Do you want to be set free? Then come, follow me.

This man knew nothing of Jesus. He had no idea that this question was really an offer. He responded, "Sir, I have no one to put me into the pool." His answer almost sounds like an admission of defeat: *What does it matter if I want to be healed? It's never going to happen. I'm not just sick, I'm sick and alone.* There was no proclamation of faith in Jesus' ability to heal, just the words of a tired man near despair. But while Jesus sometimes required faith of those he healed, faith wasn't strictly necessary for the miracles to take place. Here, he just wanted to give something beautiful to a suffering man. So he told him, "Rise, take up your mat, and walk."

Mt 9:27–31
Jn 9

Immediately, the man obeyed. He took with him his mat, a reminder of what he'd been saved from, and walked away. He had no further conversation with Jesus at that point, so shocked was he by this turn of fate. As the man was testing out his newfound strength, Jesus slipped off through the crowd.

And then John tells us that it was the Sabbath. Jesus might easily have avoided a major conflict by telling the man *not* to take his mat with him. He might have waited until the next day to offer this healing. Instead, he deliberately provoked his opponents, inviting the authorities in Jerusalem to join their less influential peers throughout Galilee in condemning him for his willingness to do good on the Sabbath.

John generally uses the word *Jews* in reference to the Jewish adversaries of Jesus. Despite John's usage, we will avoid using the phrase "the Jews" as a name for Jesus' opponents, knowing that for centuries John's terminology was deliberately misunderstood in order to support antisemitism. Most of the people in the Gospels were Jewish, both friend and foe of Jesus. "The Jews," then, would include Peter, Mary Magdalene, the Blessed Mother, and the children brought to Jesus as well as the Sadducees, the scribes, and the Pharisees (both hostile and sympathetic). It was these opponents of Jesus who stopped the formerly paralyzed man as he was carrying his mat. It was unlawful to do such a thing on the Sabbath. The man defended himself: *If the man who healed me told me to carry my mat, I'm going to carry my mat. His power clearly trumps yours.*

But he didn't know who Jesus was, nor does he seem to have sought him out afterwards. Instead, Jesus came to find him, with a warning: "Do not sin any more, so that nothing worse may happen to you."

It would be easy to read this as a connection between sin and suffering, a claim that suffering is sent as a punishment for sin. Yet, as we will see later in the Gospel, the story of the
Jn 9:1–3 man born blind makes it clear that this isn't true. Instead, Jesus is presenting the consequences of sin as something worse than thirty-eight years of debilitating illness. It's as though he's saying, *You think you know what it is to have suffered. Believe me, the years of pain you experienced are nothing compared with the consequences of sin. Please. You've been set free from illness. Live in freedom from sin, too.*

It couldn't have come as a surprise to the religious authorities that it was Jesus who had healed the man. Their hearts hardened, they looked at this man who had been healed of nearly forty years of affliction and had no joy at what God had done, only criticism over how he had done it.

Jesus answered them, "My Father is at work until now, so I am at work." Many of Jesus' contemporaries believed
that even though God rested on the seventh day, he still con- Gn 2:2
tinued to work: creating life, judging, and holding the world in being. When Jesus made this statement, then, it wasn't merely a defense of his good deeds on the Sabbath. It was implicitly a claim to be equal to the Father. Rather than explaining away their concerns, Jesus deliberately exacerbated the situation.

Each one of these Sabbath disputes pits generosity against hardheartedness. There was no dissolution of the Sabbath here, only an exhortation to use the Sabbath as the Father does: as an opportunity for rest, yes, but also for mercy and charity. The Sabbath was designed as a gift, most especially for the poor who would otherwise have had no relief from the manual labor by which they lived. That Jesus so frequently provoked this same conflict demonstrates that he had come to restore right religion, to clear away those traditions of men that kept men from the Father, from joy and Mk 7:8
rest and the peace offered by God. It wasn't just his saving death that was necessary but also his teaching, that we might understand how we are to live.

He could, perhaps, have managed to do this without continuously needling the men who had the power to hand him over to be executed, but he was never concerned with preserving his life — at least not past his appointed time. And truly, the wisdom of Jesus makes everyone uncomfortable, saint and sinner alike. Perhaps his repeated "Sabbath-breaking" was a deliberate attempt to make some of those men so uncomfortable that they listened. The Good News doesn't always sound good to those who have sated themselves on the world, the flesh, or the devil — or merely on themselves. Perhaps Jesus provoked them so that they would be saved. Uncomfortable as those repeated exchanges must have been, they were worth it if they saved even one soul.

48. Jesus Speaks of His Nature and His Power: John 5:19–47

From here, the one who was redefining the way his people observed the Sabbath chose to double down on his audacious claims. He said that he, a man, gives life, that he judges souls, that he deserves the same honor as the Father. Moreover, he told his followers that believing in him is the source of eternal life. Jesus here claimed to have life *in himself*, an
Ex 3:14 echo of God's name revealed to Moses: I am who am. This divine title declares that God is the ground of all being, that he is existence itself; here, the Good Shepherd made the same claim for himself.

Such a series of statements couldn't have passed without comment. Jesus was proclaiming blasphemy upon blasphemy, and before the Jerusalem Pharisees! Given the lack of recorded response, it's possible that John collected a group of sayings here that may not all have been spoken at that time. Or perhaps Jesus continued to preach as angry members of his audience stalked off. In any event, the claims he made here shed significant light on his divinity and on the nature of the Trinity.

Jesus again used his preferred title for himself: Son of Man. Here, his use of the term made it abundantly clear that this title is a claim of divinity. *Because* he is the Son of Man (the one coming on the clouds to take his throne
Dn 7:13 beside the Father), he is the one who judges souls. For those who have ears to hear, there is no mistaking the assertion here: He is divine, and at the sound of his voice, the dead
Ez 37:1–14 will be raised. Elijah raised the dead by speaking the word of the Lord; the Son of Man will raise the dead by the power of his own word.

Jesus closed this complex discourse by leveling an accusation at his listeners: "You accept praise from one another and do not seek the praise that comes from the only God."

This was at the heart of his disputations with the religious elite. He didn't object to their stringent adherence to the law, nor even to the many additional rules they'd established for themselves. Jesus was concerned about their motivations. These men — not every Pharisee, but many of those who agitated against him — weren't obeying the law because they desired to please God. They were trying to impress other people or even just themselves. Their righteousness was external, rooted in pride or vanity.

That's the reason they were so often unable to extend mercy or to be compassionate: They saw religion as a matter of external practice, not a handing over of the heart to God. When we live like this, congratulating ourselves on Rosaries recited and donations made without seeking the Father and giving him our lives, we, too, become clanging gongs and clashing cymbals, empty noise that gives no praise to God. 1 Cor 13:1
The good works we do lose their merit when performed for love of ourselves and not for love of God.

Jesus added insult to injury with his final remarks: "If you had believed Moses, you would have believed me." These outwardly religious Jews saw themselves above all as men of Moses, men who knew and followed the law of Moses, who were seeking to live in the image of Moses. But many were missing the heart of the matter. They may have been obedient to the rituals Moses prescribed, but they didn't live with openness to the will of God as Moses had tried to do. They didn't seek God's face. If they had truly lived as Moses lived, they would have been able to recognize Jesus as the Holy One of God.

It's a further reminder to contemporary Christians how important it is to read not just the Gospels but the entirety of the Bible. We cannot understand the life of Christ or the words of Paul or the promises of Revelation without knowing how God had already worked in the world up to that point. "If you do not believe his writings," Jesus asked, "how will you believe my words?" The more we understand the typology of the Old Testament, the prophecies pointing to

Jesus, the culture and worldview presented by the Hebrew Scriptures, the more we will accept Jesus not just as Lord but as Bridegroom, Messiah, and King.

Chapter Fifteen

Followers Sent Out on Mission

49. Jesus and Beelzebul: Matthew 12:22–32; Mark 3:20–30; *Luke 11:14–23*

Nobody could deny that Jesus was doing unexplainable things. Clearly people were being healed and demons cast out. So if his adversaries wanted to oppose him, it wasn't an option to deny the miracles. Instead, they claimed that his power came from the Evil One. These accusations would continue to be made in Jewish circles long after his death: In the Babylonian Talmud (a collection of rabbinic sayings compiled between the third and fifth centuries), Jesus is said to have practiced sorcery — the only possible explanation for all his mighty deeds if one refuses to accept his divinity.

As Jesus continued to cast out demons, people began to wonder if he was truly the Messiah, the Son of David. To quash such rumors, his opponents claimed — not for the first time — that he liberated the possessed not by the power
of God but by the power of Beelzebul, a name used for Satan. Mt 9:34
Mark situates this in the context of Jesus' conflict with his relatives, saying that they had come to seize him, thinking him to be out of his mind.

Jesus wasn't interested in being the subject of such gossip

muttered behind his back. He called the scribes in, insisting on talking face-to-face, and pointed out the flaw in their logic: If he was casting out demons by Satan's power, then Satan was working against himself and wouldn't last long. And if they could accuse him of casting out demons by Beelzebul, he could return the favor. Who was to say their exorcisms weren't calling on Satan's power as well?

"But if it is by the finger of God that [I] drive out demons, then the kingdom of God has come upon you." Jesus' use of the unusual term "finger of God" is reminiscent of two moments in the story of Moses. First, when even Pharaoh's magicians recognized that the plagues had been wrought by
Ex 8:15 the finger of God, and second, when the ten commandments
Ex 31:18; Dt 9:10 were written in stone by the finger of God. This episode began with the people calling Jesus the Son of David. *Yes*, he implied, *and also the new Moses.* Add to that his casual men-
Dn 2:44 tion of Daniel's kingdom of God, and Jesus has responded to their accusations with a clear assertion that he has been sent by the Father for the liberation of all peoples.

When Jesus followed that with "whoever is not with me is against me, and whoever does not gather with me scatters," it reads like an ultimatum, a line in the sand for those who set themselves up in opposition to him. Jesus aligned himself with David, Moses, and Daniel, and his adversaries had to choose: They could join Jesus or stand against all the heroes of the Old Testament. It wasn't even enough to cease their hostilities towards Jesus; if they didn't work alongside him, they were choosing to fight on the side of Beelzebul. By attributing to the devil the work of the Holy Spirit, they were joining forces with Satan and risking their immortal souls.

This is the blasphemy against the Holy Spirit that Jesus speaks of here, the unforgivable sin: not merely to deny the Holy Spirit's divinity, as any number of saints did before their conversions, but to remain obstinate in that denial, to refuse repentance and the mercy that reaches out to the penitent. It was this sin of final impenitence with which Jesus' interlocutors were flirting. Jesus warned them that if they continued to ignore every prompting the Spirit gave them to acknowledge his divinity, they ran the risk of partnering with the devil and forming hearts so hard that they would never be open to repentance and salvation, never able to return to the Lord. Essentially, the only sin that can't be forgiven is the sin of refusing to ask forgiveness. Every other sin can be washed away by the blood of Christ. 2 Chr 36:13

We can also hear in this warning the deep love of God the Son for God the Holy Spirit. Jesus listened to them telling lies about him, shaking his head at their ignorance and worrying for their souls. But the moment they made accusations against the Spirit of God, by whom Jesus cast out demons, he was done. *Say what you like about me*, he might have growled, *It's fine. I'll forgive you. But you leave the Holy Spirit out of this*. Obviously, there was no lack of control, but it bears considering. We often meditate on Jesus' love for the Father, but he loved the Spirit with a love just as all-encompassing. Do we?

50. The Sign of Jonah: *Matthew 12:38–42*; Luke 11:29–32

In response to this warning (bordering on a threat) and Jesus' subsequent declaration that by their words they would be condemned, the scribes and Pharisees had the audacity to demand a sign. Never mind the healing of the withered hand that had occasioned this controversy, they wanted something more. If Jesus really was the Messiah, they wanted him to prove it, right then, on their terms. Mt 12:9–14

Jesus sighed from the depths of his spirit, exhausted by the persistence of their unbelief and justly angry at their refusal to acknowledge the many, many signs he had already performed. "An evil and unfaithful generation seeks a sign," he said, though *unfaithful* might be translated better as *adulterous*. The people of Israel, called apart from all peoples to be the bride of God, had sought other gods. Even these men who prided themselves on their fidelity to the law weren't Hos 2:21–22; Is 54:5; 62:4–5 worshipping the Father when they washed and prayed and sacrificed; they were worshipping themselves. Had they truly been seeking the Father, they would have considered Jesus' claims prayerfully rather than attacking him at every possibility.

It was their adulterous nature that made them seek a sign,
that made their relationship with Jesus like their relationship
with the Father: one of transactions, not of love. Thus Jesus
said of their generation, "But no sign will be given it except
Jon 3:3–5 the sign of Jonah." Luke stops here, leaving those listening to
wonder what exactly the sign of Jonah was. Jesus and Jonah
had both preached to the Gentiles — was that all he meant?

Matthew makes it more clear: "Just as Jonah was in the
belly of the whale three days and three nights, so will the
Son of Man be in the heart of the earth three days and three
Jon 2:1 nights." It's the only Scripture that Jesus quotes that directly
Mt 16:21; 17:22– points to his resurrection. He foretells his dying and rising
23; 20:17–19 elsewhere, but this passage is the only allusion he makes to
an Old Testament foreshadowing of his resurrection.

It's a powerful comparison, mostly because anyone can
see how much worse Jonah looks by comparison to Jesus.
Jonah was called by God and ran away, refusing to be an
Jon 1:1–3 instrument of mercy to the hated Ninevites. When he was
finally persuaded to relent, he preached reluctantly, so half-
heartedly that the Ninevites' conversion could only have
come by a miracle, one even greater than Jonah's salvation
Jon 3:4 by a whale. But convert they did — from the animals in
the stalls to the king on his throne, they wore sackcloth and
begged the Lord to have pity on them. God, "who wills ev-
1 Tm 2:4 eryone to be saved," delighted in their miraculous repentance
and extended his mercy to them. Jonah, on the other hand,
was furious, praying for death because he would rather die
Jon 4:1–3 than see the Ninevites saved.

Even Jesus' most obstinate opponents couldn't have denied that Jesus, with his powerful preaching, compassion, and healing miracles, was a far better prophet than Jonah, even if they thought he was working for someone other than the God of Abraham, Isaac, and Jacob. Truly, Jesus is the antithesis of Jonah. But at Jonah's preaching, the accursed Ninevites repented, while many of God's chosen people who heard Jesus turned their backs.

Jesus then compared himself with Solomon, the son of David, whose wisdom was famed throughout the earth while his virtue waned to the point of destroying the unity of the twelve tribes of Israel. Again, Jesus far surpassed Solomon, but Solomon's wisdom had converted the Queen of Sheba, while wisdom incarnate was ignored.

1 Kgs 11:4–13; Neh 13:26

1 Kgs 10:1–3

If the Gentiles of old had listened to such weak and sinful men as Jonah and Solomon, the Jews of Jesus' time had no excuse not to listen to him. They would have their sign when he rose from the dead. Even then, he knew, many would continue in their disbelief.

51. Jesus Sends Out the Twelve: *Matthew 10:5–15*; Mark 6:7–13; Luke 9:1–6

The story of Jesus' public ministry up to this point shows him surrounded by followers — particularly the Twelve — as he preached and healed and responded to one criticism after another. He modeled compassion and generosity for those he had called, spoke to them about the kingdom, called them to holiness, and finally sent them out.

This was a group of ordinary, uneducated men, with little to recommend them other than Jesus' good opinion. They wouldn't have been at the top of anybody's list of revolutionaries, prophets, or miracle-workers. But, as the saying goes, God doesn't call the qualified, he qualifies the called. And now he filled them with power they had never imagined. With a word, he gave them authority over demons and power to cure every disease. He began a pattern that continues to this day, as God uses human instruments to bring healing, peace, and salvation to his people. No longer mere disciples (followers of a teacher), they were now apostles (the ones who are sent).

Acts 4:13

This commissioning must have been thrilling for the

Twelve, who were being sent out to heal, anoint, cast out demons, and proclaim the Good News. They weren't sent as emissaries of a great king, though, with caravans of supplies, bodyguards, and courtiers. As disciples of a homeless man, they traveled simply, making themselves entirely dependent on the hospitality of those whom they served. They carried no money, nor even a change of clothes. When someone took them in, they were to stay in that home, regardless of what better offers may have been made once they'd impressed the local gentry. Everything about this mission demanded humility.

It was necessary. When you give a man the power to work miracles (or to preach or teach or throw a ball or play an instrument), it's very easy for him to become convinced that his gift is his own, something of which to be proud. Jesus sent the Twelve out in pairs for accountability and in poverty so that their new power might not destroy their souls.

They would be admired, of course: "How beautiful
upon the mountains / are the feet of the one bringing good
news, / Announcing peace, bearing good news (*euangelion*),
Is 52:7 / announcing salvation, saying to Zion, 'Your God is King!'"
This was exactly the mission of the Twelve: to announce the
good news of the kingdom, brought about by the God who
had come to save them.

But they would also be hated, preaching the message Jesus had given them. Even crying out "The kingdom of heaven is at hand!" would make them enemies. Jesus protected them from discouragement as well as pride, warning them that some wouldn't listen. When he told them to shake the dust from their feet, he was reminding them that the opinions of others don't define us. So often we encounter opposition in serving Jesus, but instead of shaking off the dust, we allow it to cling to us. We replay frustrating encounters in our heads or believe the ugly things spoken against us. We convince ourselves that only we can save these folks, and we ruin ourselves trying to speak the name of Jesus to people who will only ever be able to hear the Good News from someone else. We beat ourselves up or we elect ourselves their Messiah. Jesus told the Twelve to let go of all that, to leave their opponents to him. We need to do the same.

It's telling that Jesus instructed his apostles not to go to the Gentiles or the Samaritans. His own habit was to heal indiscriminately; the early Church, too, would soon realize that they were being sent to all nations. Here, though, Jesus had a group of Jewish men who didn't yet understand what the kingdom of heaven was, even as they were proclaiming it. For their protection, and (perhaps) for the protection of the pagans and Samaritans they might have encountered, he told them to limit themselves to Israel. After he was lifted up, he would draw all men to himself. Then they would go out to all nations. For now, it was good to leave the training wheels on.

Acts 10:34–35, 47–48

Jn 12:32

Some of the Twelve may have been delighted with these instructions. Peter, for one, must have been eager to work wonders like Jesus had. Others may have been more apprehensive, unsure about leaving Jesus' side, particularly when he warned them of the coming persecutions. Surely Matthew the former tax collector was worried about how they were expected to travel with no money or even a walking stick. And though they had spent months with Jesus, there was so much they still didn't understand. What on earth would they say when they preached? But we read of no objections, just obedience. After some months of following Jesus, they had begun to see how Providence is to be trusted.

52. Courage under Persecution: *Matthew 10:16–36*; Mark 13:9–13; Luke 12:2–15, *49–53*

While Jesus knew that his disciples would be relatively unharmed on their first excursion, this mission was to set the pattern for later missions, when every word they spoke in his name would bring the hangman's noose nearer. He spoke to them of persecution, of the suffering that they would encounter because of their allegiance to him. Like sheep into the midst of wolves he would send them, but he himself was their shepherd. And when they were brought before their persecutors — as they inevitably would be — the Spirit would speak through them.

We who look back with the benefit of hindsight can see saint after saint who sang her way to the scaffold or preached his greatest sermon from his cross. Saints Ignatius of Antioch and Perpetua and Felicity and Genesius and Edmund Campion and Margaret Ward and Paul Miki and Agatha Kim and Charles Lwanga and José Sánchez del Río all went bravely to torturous deaths and allowed the Spirit to turn their blood into the seed of the Church, as did the apostles who had listened to Jesus' words. Spurred on by his encouragement, they refused to fear the one who could kill the body because they trusted the one who had promised to save their souls.

What would seem to the world to be a tragedy, the torture and slaughter of Christians, would instead be an opportunity for Jesus' followers to act as witnesses — to go as faithful sheep preaching the Good Shepherd to the wolves Jesus also loved. What they had first spoken in whispers would be proclaimed before kings and emperors, in the courtroom and the arena. Even Jesus' warning that they should flee from a town where they were persecuted became an avenue for the evangelization of the world. Later, in the Acts of the
Acts 8:1 Apostles, the persecution of Christians in Jerusalem led them
to go out to Judea and Samaria and ultimately to the ends
Acts 1:8 of the earth. In God's economy, the horrors of persecution
are never wasted, whether in Jerusalem, Nagasaki, or Mosul.

It wasn't just government officials Jesus warned about; the very family members of those who followed him would become a threat. Many of us today live without fear of state persecution but experience mockery and abuse at the hands of those we love most because we choose to live marked by the cross of Christ. But in suffering persecution from those we love, we join with our Savior who went before us, the dis-
Mt 5:11–12 ciples becoming like the master. Blessed are we.

After all these warnings, Jesus spoke tenderly to his beloved followers. He's recorded as speaking these words to his apostles, but they might easily have been spoken another time, to a disconsolate child or a bereft widow as he wiped the tears from their cheeks. "Are not two sparrows sold for a small coin?" he asked. "Yet not one of them falls to the ground without your Father's knowledge." The Greek is vague here; it might equally be translated "without your Father's consent" or "outside your Father's care." The text is expressing a deep attentiveness, a degree of care so intense that the Father runs his fingers through our hair to count each strand. "Even all the hairs of your head are counted. So do not be afraid; you are worth more than many sparrows." These are words to hide in your heart, words to memorize and recite when the devil's lies begin to overwhelm you. Imagine Jesus speaking these words to your broken, fearful, weary heart, wiping the tears from your eyes. Imagine the love in his voice, the strength with which he forbids you to fear. It's not much of a compliment, being worth more than many sparrows, but when taken all together, when spoken from the mouth of God, it's enough to give the believer the strength to go on. Followed by Jesus' promise to stand beside those who have claimed him as Lord, to acknowledge them before his heavenly Father, these words of Jesus become fortification for the weary soul.

Jesus may have come to bring peace to the heart, but not to the earth. He came to set the world ablaze with a fire of love, of purification, and of judgment. He came to set fires in the hearts of men, that they might never be lukewarm in his service. "I have come to set the earth on fire, and how Rv 3:16
I wish it were already blazing!" This was not a wish but a commission: Jesus has called all his followers to live for him and set the world on fire. But in the process, he warned that we would face division and the sword, a statement as true now as it was during his earthly ministry. We who make the Sign of the Cross will live in the shadow of the cross, in our families just as much as in the public square. Even in a Christian country or a Christian family, there will be suffering for those who are faithful. We follow a crucified God and can expect nothing less. Still, the Spirit is sovereign, and he will

speak in and through us. He will strengthen and encourage us. And even in our persecution, God will be glorified.

We tend to assume that those who followed Jesus through Galilee and Judea were so awestruck by his teaching that they were transformed and equipped to be great saints. But as often as not, they seemed to be waiting for Jesus to stop preaching so they could ask for what they really wanted. Here, Jesus was warning of the suffering to come, promising the gift of the indwelling Holy Spirit, and waxing poetic on the love of the Father. Perhaps most of them were entranced by his words, but one man was just waiting for a gap in Jesus' preaching so he could interrupt and insist that the teacher support him in his quest for money. Never one to lose an opportunity to teach, Jesus asked, "Who appointed me as your judge and arbitrator?"

We hear that question and wonder at it. The Father did, of course. But the language Jesus used was deliberate, a refer-
Ex 2:14 ence to the challenge posed to Moses by one of the Israelites before it was revealed that God had chosen Moses to lead his people out of slavery. Jesus, the new Moses, had the authority to enforce this man's request, having been appointed judge and arbitrator by the Father. Saint Stephen would later refer-
Acts 7:35 ence this same question, reminding the people that when it had been asked of Moses, it was their ruler and deliverer they were rejecting, just as God's people would later reject their ruler and deliverer, God incarnate in Jesus Christ.

But as his question (his allusion) hung in the air, Jesus moved to respond to the man's appeal, not with a judgment as to the law but with an exhortation: Be wary of greed. This man's heart must have been greatly consumed by avarice if such was his response to the warnings and promises and compassion of the preceding verses. God, preserve us from such obsessions. God, set us afire with love for you instead.

53. Dependence on God: Matthew 6:25–34; *Luke 12:22–34*

The greatest danger of wealth is that it robs us of our need to trust God — until we're faced with a problem that wealth

can't solve. But while poverty leaves us with no illusions about the fact that we rest firmly in the hands of Providence, worry then threatens to overwhelm us. So immediately after warning of the dangers of wealth, Jesus commanded his poor and persecuted brethren not to worry. Not about their lives, their bodies, their food, or their clothing. Saint Paul
would go on to forbid anxiety and command joy, taking as Phil 4:4–7
his model the Suffering Servant who trusted in the Father and expected his followers to do the same.

This is not, of course, a condemnation of clinical anxiety. Jesus doesn't look askance at those who struggle with mental illness any more than he would denigrate people with a disability or a chronic illness. This is an invitation to choose to trust even when we don't feel trusting, to cast our
cares on the Lord again and again. When the command not 1 Pt 5:7; Ps 55:23
to be anxious gives us more anxiety because we feel that even our anxiety is a failure, we have to refuse to read these passages as though God were saying, *What is wrong with you? I said not to be anxious!* Instead, hear his gentle, soothing reassurance: *Hey, now. You're OK. There's nothing to worry about. Don't be anxious, love. I've got this. I'm right here.*

Again, we're given birds as a model, creatures who plan Mt 10:29–31
to some extent as they build their nests and who work to procure food but are never troubled over plans for the future, living as they do in the now. "How much more important are you than birds!" Jesus insists, an echo of his proclamation
some fifteen verses earlier in Luke. Lk 12:7

The next verse is rather more pointed: "Can any of you by worrying add a moment to your life-span?" Even if the analogy of ravens didn't resonate (given their lack of rent payments and resumés), we have to acknowledge this point: Worrying accomplishes nothing. Planning can be important (though, ultimately, we have no control over the future), but worry only paralyzes us, convincing us that we have to take care of all the particulars of a situation. When we worry, we make ourselves God, only without his wisdom or power.

He continued, "If even the smallest things are beyond

your control, why are you anxious about the rest?" This command against anxiety is ultimately an invitation to trust
Rom 8:32 that the God who sent his Son to die for us loves us enough to take care of us, even if not in the way we would expect.
Rom 6:3–4; Gal 2:20 When we died to ourselves in baptism, we offered our lives to Christ, that he might live in us. We made him Lord of our lives. That means trusting him not just with our ultimate salvation but with finances and family planning and traffic jams. The God who had the wisdom to send his Son to the cross and call it *Good* Friday is at work in all of our circumstances, however hopeless they may seem.

It's as if Jesus puts his hands on our shoulders as we panic over one thing or another and says, *Stop. Breathe. Look at the incredible world your Father made. If he could create the universe, he can get you a flight to Akron. Or not. He knows what he is about. Do not worry anymore.* Stop allowing the things of this world to consume you, he says, and seek the kingdom. If your ultimate goal is holiness, God will give you that and more besides. If holiness is secondary to comfort or success or status, in the end you will find that you have none of what you sought.

Again, the tenderness of Jesus comes out: "Do not be afraid any longer, little flock, for your Father is pleased to give you the kingdom." And the kingdom is all that matters. God can work all things for our good, whatever may come. Even our death may be an avenue for grace, for us and for those who love us. The only tragedy is sin. When failures (real or imagined) threaten to strangle us with anxiety, a kingdom perspective makes it possible to live in the freedom Christ offers. "This may be bad," we can say, "but it is not
Rom 8:28 irreparably bad. My God works all things for good."

In our age of a thousand stresses, where clinical anxiety is an epidemic, Jesus' attitude might seem trite, even naïve. "Do not worry about tomorrow," he says. "Tomorrow will take care of itself. Sufficient for a day is its own evil." This, in the face of bills past due and refugees and infertility and abortion and racism and internet trolls. How can we possibly not worry?

Ultimately, it comes down to this: He wants us to know who we are and whose we are. We are his. We are unceasingly, inestimably loved. When worry and anxiety threaten to overwhelm us, the only solution is to return to this truth, to rest in the Father's embrace. If it's true that we belong to him, that he's promised to take care of us, then worry is senseless. So we pay our bills and make career plans and vote and do all the other things our neighbors do to prepare for the future, but when our plans are derailed, we turn to him. "Jesus, I trust in you," we say, hoping that it will become true even if it doesn't yet feel true. We keep the kingdom as our goal and trust him for the rest.

Conclusion

It's a fitting place to pause, this commissioning and exhortation to trust in God. Like the apostles, we have been called, formed, and sent out. Like the apostles, we often feel we have no idea what we're doing. But with them, we've fixed our eyes on Jesus, which makes it possible (if still not easy) to trust him. And though they have the benefit of having walked and eaten and laughed with him, we, too, have known him. We've meditated on the darkness of a world without him and the radiant light his life brought into that darkness. We've gazed at his tiny divine face as a baby, wept with him as he fled his homeland, and rejoiced when he returned. With the shepherds and the magi, with Simeon and Anna, we've worshipped the Christ child, though even now we wonder if we truly grasp what it means that God became man.

We've gasped at the voice of the Father calling him beloved, and — perhaps — we have begun to follow. Maybe, like Andrew and John, a glimpse of him was enough to make us want to be his. Maybe we needed a miracle (like Peter) or a concrete call out of a life of sin (like Matthew). Maybe with Nathanael we came grudgingly, uninterested in his claims at first but captivated once we truly met him. Like the hemorrhaging woman, we may have been desperate for healing or (like Photina) desperate to hide.

However we came to Jesus, we've spent hours and hours

now meditating on him, imagining his tone of voice and his
expressions, trying to see what it was about him that brought
the sinful woman weeping to his feet while his childhood
friends tried to throw him off a cliff. We've heard him call
us to holiness, blanching at times when we realize just what
it costs to follow a crucified God. But whatever he's asked,
he's given far more — even at this point in the story, when
he hasn't yet walked the hill of Calvary and handed himself
Jer 31:3 over for us. Over and over, he's spoken of his age-old love,
his deep desire for us to be entirely his. Over and over, he's
promised us that he wants us. Exactly as we are.

This is where we leave him, for the time being. He has
begun to show us who he is and who we are in him. Already
he's moving toward the cross, though nobody but Mary
knows it yet. In the next volume, we'll begin to hear him
speak of his coming passion and death. We'll see him set his
Lk 9:51 face resolutely toward Jerusalem, where his anguish will win
our salvation. In the third and final volume of this series,
we'll stand by in horror as he offers his life for each of us as
though there were only one of us. And then — wonder of
wonders — we'll witness the empty tomb, touch his risen
body, eat and walk and speak with him again.

For now, we join the apostles in setting out with his
name on our lips and his joy in our heart. Surrounded by the
Heb 12:1 cloud of witnesses who have shown us in this volume what it
is to follow Jesus, we seek to trust him in the midst of uncertainty, in the midst of anguish, in the midst of love and loss and loneliness. We fix our eyes on Jesus. We run or trudge or crawl after him. And we trust that he is with us even when we can't see his face.

Acknowledgments

I began dreaming about this book in 2017 and writing it in early 2018 — long before my other books, which went on to be published first. I hadn't particularly dreamed of writing a book until I dreamed of writing this book, and every book I've written since then has been, at its core, an effort to open doors so that this book would get a chance.

I should, I suppose, thank this book for all the others. But more than that, I should thank the people who encouraged and supported me in the years that it took to bring this work to the world.

Thanks to Grandmother and Grandfather who gave me my Bible at my first holy Communion — the Bible I've read every day for the last twenty-two years (and most days for the five years before that).

Thanks to the Key-Vranish family for giving me a space to squat as I wrestled with the first draft of this work. Truly this book wouldn't exist if it weren't for your generosity.

Thanks to Katherine for the computer I wrote this book on. Also for everything else.

Thanks to Kayla, to whom I sent word count updates every single night and who always responded with consummate enthusiasm. Thanks to Christina and Anamaría, who were genuinely excited about this project when so many other people just smiled politely while I talked about it. Your enthusiasm gave me more joy (and energy) than you can know. Thanks to Aaron for the heresy proofread and to John Paul for asking after this book every time you saw me for the last several years. Thanks to Rachael for wanting so badly to read it, to Anjanette for believing in this project and fighting for it, and to Mary Beth for always making my writing better, my meaning clearer, and my exhortations gentler. Thanks to Dr. Scott Powell and Fr. Peter Mussett, whose podcast was an inestimable gift as I was preparing this book.

Thanks to the thousands and thousands of people who have shown up to my talks or listened to my podcasts or read my social media posts or come to my Bible studies or sat in my office asking about Scripture. The Holy Spirit has taught me so much when I've been trying to teach you, and I know this book would be far shallower if you hadn't given me a platform from which to (try to) let him speak through me.

Thanks to Saint Jerome, Saint Paul, and Our Lady, Lover of the Word, the patrons of this work whose prayers made every word possible.

Recommended Reading

Ignatius Catholic Study Bible

Kenneth E. Bailey: *Jesus Through Middle Eastern Eyes: Cultural Studies in the Gospels*

John Bergsma: *New Testament Basics for Catholics*

Alfred Edersheim: *The Life and Times of Jesus the Messiah*

Peter Kreeft: *You Can Understand the Bible: A Practical and Illuminating Guide to Each Book in the Bible*

Göran Larsson: *Bound for Freedom: The Book of Exodus in Jewish and Christian Traditions*

Erasmo Leiva-Merikakis: *Fire of Mercy, Heart of the Word* (four volumes)

Frank Sheed: *To Know Christ Jesus*

Brant Pitre: *The Case for Jesus: The Biblical and Historical Evidence for Christ*

Brant Pitre: *Jesus the Bridegroom: The Greatest Love Story Ever Told*

Brant Pitre: *Jesus and the Jewish Roots of the Eucharist: Unlocking the Secrets of the Last Supper*

Patrick Henry Reardon: *Christ in the Psalms*

St. Thomas Aquinas: *The Catena Aurea*

Peter S. Williamson, Mary Healy, and Mark Giszczak, editors: *Catholic Commentary on Sacred Scripture* (seventeen volumes)

Pope Benedict XVI: *Jesus of Nazareth* (three volumes)

Study Guide

These questions are only a guide. You and your group may find you have enough to discuss from the text (and accompanying Scripture readings) without ever needing to use these questions. Before you look at the specific questions offered here, begin by opening up the discussion more generally. Try questions like this:

- What stuck out to you?
- Was there anything you'd never considered before?
- Which Old Testament connection did you find most striking?
- Where did you disagree with the author?
- What point(s) do you plan to take to prayer?

Then feel free to move to the questions written for each chapter.

Introduction and Chapter One

1. What has been your experience of reading Scripture in the past? If you have experience reading the Bible, what approaches have you tried? What have you found helpful?
2. Does this description of God the Son as distant resonate with you? Why or why not? Have you had any experiences that made the person of Jesus feel close?
3. Have you thought about Jesus' personality before? His physical appearance? How do you imagine him? What has affected this image that you have?
4. As you read John 1:1–18, what did you see in these verses that you had not

seen before? What questions do you still have?
5. What is your usual reaction when you hear a genealogy read aloud at Mass? Does this reflection help you to see more value in these readings? Open your Bible to either Matthew's or Luke's genealogy. Highlight or underline the names you recognize. What did you find most interesting about Jesus' genealogies?
6. Are there unanswered prayers in your life that you continue to pray for? Have you been tempted to give up hoping, even if you still pray? How does Zechariah's experience speak to this in your life?
7. Are there prayers that went unanswered in the past for which you're now grateful, whether they were answered after a fruitful delay or never answered at all? How does this experience affect your approach to unanswered prayers now?
8. Were the Old Testament references in this chapter familiar to you? If yes, which ones stood out to you? Choose one paragraph and dig into the Old Testament references as a group.

Chapter Two

1. What is one surprising thing you learned about the Annunciation or one detail you saw in a new way?
2. How might meditating on Mary's fiat (her unconditional yes to God) be helpful in your prayer life right now?
3. The tradition suggests either that Joseph felt himself unworthy to be the foster father of Jesus or that he doubted Mary's story. Have you heard both these theories? Which one do you find more compelling? Why? What value can you find in the other as well?
4. Elizabeth's reference to Judith and Jael invites us to reconsider our image of Mary. How have you imagined Mary's personality in the past? How might this encounter in Luke's Gospel lead you to conceive of her in a different way, while being faithful to Scripture and Tradition? How do Jael and Judith inform your understanding of "biblical femininity"?
5. Dig into the references to Old Testament passages about the Ark of the Covenant. What do these passages tell us about Mary?
6. What line from the Magnificat makes you most uncomfortable? Why do you think that is?
7. Have you, like Zechariah, had a moment or a season when you felt God asking you to trust him even though he seemed distant or silent? Were you able to do so? Why or why not?

8. Study the Canticle of Zechariah (Lk 1:68–79). What is Zechariah proclaiming here about Jesus? How do you need these promises to be fulfilled in your life?

Chapter Three

1. What elements of the Christmas story struck you as you read? Why?
2. How do you feel about meditating on the Passion while studying the Nativity? What Christmas hymns can you think of that reflect the unity between these two events?
3. Why do you think Jesus' birth was announced first to shepherds?
4. The biblical and historical contexts imbue the term *euangelion* or "good news" with profound significance. What has your experience of hearing and embracing the good news of the Gospel been? Is there anything in your life or experience that prevents you from delighting in the knowledge of God's saving love? How can you begin to surrender that to Jesus?
5. Reread the last two paragraphs of section 8 [page 235]. Does this idea of the personal love of God who came to earth to save *you* resonate with you?
6. What do you think about the Eastern Christian legend about Simeon? Whether or not it's true, how can this legend teach you to long for Jesus in a more powerful way?

Chapter Four

1. What roles of Jesus do the magi's gifts of gold, frankincense, and myrrh highlight? Why do you think the Gospel points out these three roles particularly? Which of these roles speaks most strongly to your spiritual life? How can you offer similar gifts to the Lord?
2. Reflect on the difficulties the Holy Family faced when they fled to Egypt. Do you think the instruction "Flee to Egypt" was even harder for them than "Flee to Syria" or "Flee to Arabia" would have been? Why?
3. Have you considered Mary and Joseph's grief and guilt after the Slaughter of the Innocents before? How does it make you feel to imagine Mary crying out to God in grief or even anger about this massacre? How does this image bring you consolation?
4. How do you imagine Mary and Joseph felt on their return to Judea? What good did God bring out of their time in Egypt? Does considering this help you to see how God might be working even through the difficult areas in your life?
5. What strikes you in meditating on the finding of Jesus in the Temple? Why

do you think Jesus left his parents to remain in the Temple? What can we learn from their interaction after they found him?
6. How can we reconcile Mary's reaction to Jesus in the Temple with her sinlessness? How do the emotions we see in Mary in this episode encourage you as you deal with similar emotions?

Chapter Five

1. John the Baptist quotes Isaiah, promising an end to captivity and forgiveness of guilt. What is one way that you need this Good News proclaimed in your life right now? Have you experienced this liberation and healing in the past?
2. What do you think of this description of the Pharisees? Is it new to you? How does this understanding affect some of your previous assumptions about the gospel stories?
3. Why do you think John the Baptist asked so little of tax collectors and soldiers, who were so far from faithful adherence to God's law? Why was he so harsh with the Pharisees? How do you think he would speak to you, if you went out to meet him?
4. What does the phrase "Lamb of God" call to mind for you? What would it have called to mind for the Jewish people? What do all these layers of truth teach us about who Jesus is, especially in the mystery of his baptism?
5. What are some of the truths about Jesus revealed by his baptism? What light does this shed on the Sacrament of Baptism?
6. Take a few moments to pray, imagining the Father speaking these words over you: "This is my beloved son/daughter, with whom I am well pleased." If anything stands in the way of you imagining the Father speaking of you in this way, ask Jesus to help you surrender it to him.

Chapter Six

1. What has your experience of fasting been? How has it strengthened you, as it clearly strengthened Jesus? How has it been revelatory? If fasting from food is unwise for you given your physical or mental health, what other forms of sacrifice have you found fruitful?
2. Satan tempts Jesus with pleasure, power, and pride; which of these is hardest for you to resist? How can Jesus' response strengthen you to face these temptations?
3. Imagine yourself facing a trial from the devil. Is there a specific temptation

that you know you'd be most likely to submit to? What is it? What are two or three concrete steps you can take to resist this temptation in your everyday life?
4. When you do manage to resist temptation, is your resistance clothed in bitterness? Guilt? Fear? Pride? Something else? Why do you think that is?
5. How did Jesus fulfill the Messianic expectations of his people? How did he subvert them? Does this shed more light for you on Jesus' purpose as Messiah?
6. As you read John 1:35–42, how do you imagine this scene? What stands out to you? Why do you think Andrew and John were so drawn to Jesus?
7. When you approach Jesus, what are you looking for?
8. What resonates with you in this imagining of Nathanael's story? Is there a particular wound you need Jesus to speak healing into? Pause for a few moments to invite God to speak to you in the silence.

Chapter Seven

1. How do you react to the image of Jesus as bridegroom? Does it resonate with you? Why or why not?
2. For Mary, intercession simply involved presenting a need to Jesus, not describing the problem, outlining possible solutions, or even enlisting the aid of others. What can we learn from this model of intercession as we intercede for others?
3. Mary's last words in the Gospel are, "Do whatever he tells you." In what area of your life is this advice hardest to follow? How can Mary's motherly guidance help you?
4. Peter's mother-in-law's response to God's grace was immediate, wholehearted service. What do you think your response would be? What is one small change you can commit to that would help you imitate her?
5. Imagine the crowd of people pressing close to Jesus in search of healing. Where would you be in this crowd? What would you be doing? Bringing someone to Jesus? Shoving others out of the way to get there yourself? Stuck in the middle, or on the outskirts, helpless to get to Jesus? A few blocks over, resentful or hopeless or suspicious or self-sufficient or certain that he won't want to help you? What do you need Jesus to heal in your life right now?
6. As you read Luke's account of the rejection at Nazareth (Lk 4:16–30), how do you imagine the crowd's reactions at various points in the story? What would your reaction be?
7. Does the description of Jesus as a stranger and a sojourner resonate with you? Where do you feel this way? Has your experience with the Church made

this better or worse?

Chapter Eight

1. Like Peter, there are likely some areas of your life that you gladly hand over to Jesus and others that seem as though they ought to be your domain. Where do you struggle to give God control? What strategies can you put in place to help you surrender these issues to the Lord?
2. Peter asked for help, and his friends' eternity was changed. Do you find it easier to give or receive help? Share a story of a time when you were weak and your weakness ended up being a gift to someone else.
3. We're already seeing a pattern in the Gospel of how people bring each other to Jesus. Who are the people in your life who have brought you to God? Have you thanked them?
4. Jesus was intentional about taking time to pray in silence by himself. How can you make this happen in your life? What do you find most difficult about silent prayer? How have you found it to be necessary in your life?
5. Which Old Testament references listed in this chapter did you find most striking? Why?
6. How do you reconcile Jesus' tenderness with his fierceness? Which element of his personality figures more strongly in your experience of him? How else would you describe him?
7. Why do you think Nicodemus came to visit Jesus at night? Is there some area of your life that you only bring to Jesus under cover of darkness?
8. Why do you think John 3:16 resonates with people so strongly? Do you have a favorite Bible verse? What touches you particularly about this verse?

Chapter Nine

1. Read Matthew 5:1–12 together. Which Beatitude do you find most consoling? Which do you find most challenging? Did the imagined audience shared in this chapter shed any light on the Beatitudes for you?
2. Throughout the Sermon on the Mount, Jesus repeatedly calls his followers to holiness through observance of strict moral norms. Which of these precepts seems most radical to you? Which is hardest for you to follow?
3. Following Jesus ought to change us in a way that draws others to him. Do you know anybody whose life was so changed when they turned to Jesus that it brought other people to him as well? What happened?
4. Choose one challenge from the Sermon on the Mount to focus on for the

next week. What practical changes can you make this week in order to live out this call?

5. This interpretation of the leper's willingness to approach Jesus suggests that he saw Jesus as "safe." C. S. Lewis famously said that Aslan (his Christ figure) was not safe, "not a tame lion." What do you think Lewis meant by that? Can we view Jesus as safe to approach while also understanding that he will not leave us unchanged?

6. Does Jesus feel safe to you? Does the Church? If yes, why? If no, why not?

Chapter Ten

1. Did you know the history of the Samaritans? What questions do you have about the shape of Israel's past?

2. By some measures, Jesus' initial words to Photina could be called rude. Are you comfortable with the idea of God being rude? Do you have examples from your life of a time that God did something beautiful by going against your desires or expectations?

3. Asking about Photina's husband makes her feel excluded — until Jesus makes it clear that he still wants her. Is there something about your life that makes you feel unwanted by the Church? Has anyone helped you to feel welcomed? Is there something the other members of this group can do to support you?

4. Photina felt such healing in the eyes of Jesus that she went straight to the people who had thrown her past in her face again and again; rather than concealing it, this time she brought it up. Do you have past wounds that are so healed you don't mind talking about them? Do you think true healing is possible even if you're not able to talk freely about something?

5. Consider the image of the centurion's faith bringing joy to Jesus' heart. Can you imagine him taking that joy in your faith? Why or why not?

6. Have you ever felt unworthy of God's love? What do you wish you'd been told then to help you be truly humble rather than self-loathing?

Chapter Eleven

1. Have you had an experience of Jesus bearing your griefs and sorrows for you? What was that like?

2. Together, read Luke 9:57–62. In all honesty, would you say that you're following Jesus right now? Is there something he could ask of you that would cause you to turn back?

3. Have you ever had an experience that felt like the storm at sea — utter chaos in which God seemed to be silent and uncaring? Were you able to turn to Jesus? What did that look like?
4. In what situations are you inclined to turn to God immediately? When do you turn to him only as a last resort? What can you do to have more of the former and fewer of the latter?
5. The Gerasene demoniac's neighbors were terrified when they saw the results of Jesus' power. Is there anything about Jesus that you find frightening?
6. Why do you think Jesus asked so many people to keep silent about their experiences with him but told the former demoniac to spread the word?
7. Who are the people in your life who will rip off a roof to bring you to Jesus? For whom would you do the same? What does this look like practically?
8. Have you found yourself in a situation similar to the paralytic, where God seems to ignore your desires and bless you with something you never asked for? What's your reaction when that happens?

Chapter Twelve

1. Who are the prostitutes and tax collectors that you just can't imagine inviting into your life? What would it look like to love them as Jesus did?
2. Matthew sees his call as miraculous. Do you have a story of when you began to follow Jesus? Share it with the group.
3. What have been the roles of feasting and fasting in your life? Has either helped you to feel closer to the Lord? How?
4. When do you find prayer most natural? Most necessary? Most difficult?
5. As amazing as it was that Jesus raised the widow's son, it must have been hard for some of those whose loved ones had stayed dead. Why do you think it happens that some people get miracles and others get nothing? How have you handled these unanswered prayers in your own life?
6. Imagine being Jairus while Jesus was listening to the newly healed woman tell him the whole truth about her chronic illness. How would you have felt? Do you tend to view other people's blessings with resentment? Do you get impatient with God when he delays the answer to your prayer?
7. Jesus called the hemorrhaging woman "daughter." What relationship to God do you find most beautiful? (Son? Friend? Servant? Beloved? Bride? Brother?) Which relational image is most dominant in your spiritual life? Which is hardest to stomach?
8. What promises does God make that you respond to with scorn and cynicism?

Chapter Thirteen

1. How do you read John's questioning of Jesus? Does it seem intended to teach his students, as this book suggests? Rooted in doubt? Attempting to provoke a response, perhaps a miracle? What might different readings offer us for our meditation?
2. In what area of your life is it most difficult to let God be God?
3. Holiness often lies in the middle, where vice is a distorted excess of a virtue or an absence of that virtue. But here Jesus proposes virtue as being one extreme or the other, as opposed to a refusal to commit. Can these both be true? Discuss.
4. The sinful woman (or perhaps "the forgiven woman" is a better name) showed great love because she had been forgiven much. Are you comfortable with this idea that God can use even our sins for his glory, or does it strike you as unfair? Have you seen this kind of redemption in your own life?
5. Who do you identify with most in the story of the forgiven woman? Why?
6. Jesus traveled with Mary Magdalene, Joanna, Susanna, and "many other" women. Describe the types of women that you imagine following him. Can you "think outside the box" here? What surprising types of people could be added to your list?

Chapter Fourteen

1. What do Sundays look like for you? Do you take a weekly time of rest and worship, or is your approach to Sunday either meaningless or legalistic?
2. Have you had any meaningful experiences of the Sabbath? What practices might you adopt to make Sundays more of an opportunity to be rejuvenated?
3. What are some non-religious rituals that bring you comfort, meaning, or direction? What are some religious ones? What makes a ritual lose its meaning for you?
4. Matthew seems to be encouraging us to trust in Jesus even when we struggle to understand his teachings. What Church teachings do you struggle with? Is there something that enables you to accept them anyway?
5. Is legalism a temptation for you in any area? Or do you err more on the side of ignoring the law for the sake of doing what seems right? What would healthy balance look like?
6. This chapter highlights some of Jesus' deliberately provocative behavior. Do you think it's possible for people to imitate this contentious approach while remaining both virtuous and effective? How do you decide which battles to

pick and which to drop?

7. As you read John 5:19–47, what stood out to you? What gave you pause?

8. Jesus stresses the importance of knowing the Old Testament; what has your experience been with reading the Old Testament? Do you have favorite Old Testament books? What are they?

Chapter Fifteen

1. Have you considered Jesus' love of the Holy Spirit before? What is your relationship with the Holy Spirit like? How can Jesus' love for the Spirit inform yours?

2. Read the Book of Jonah (it's only four short chapters). How does Jonah point ahead to Jesus? How is Jesus nothing at all like Jonah?

3. Have you ever been asked to step out in faith as the apostles were? How did that go?

4. Do you find the stories of martyred saints inspiring or upsetting? How do those stories inspire you to live a holier ordinary life?

5. Read Matthew 10:29–31 slowly. What word or phrase gives you the most comfort?

6. When you read condemnations of anxiety in Scripture, how does that make you feel? Do you have any strategies to combat worry?

7. In what area of your life do you find it hardest to trust God?

8. Read Luke 12:22–34 together. Which line do you find most consoling? Most frustrating?

Topical Index

The page number indicated is the first page of the section in which the topic is featured.

A

B

C

D

E

F

G

K

L

M

N

O

P

R

S

T

U

V

W

Z

Index of Scripture References

Genesis

Exodus

Leviticus

Numbers

Deuteronomy

Joshua

Judges

Ruth

1 Samuel

2 Samuel

1 Kings

2 Kings

1 Chronicles

2 Chronicles

Ezra

Nehemiah

Tobit

Judith

Esther

1 Maccabees

2 Maccabees

Psalms

Proverbs

Song of Songs

Wisdom

Sirach

Isaiah

Jeremiah

Baruch

Ezekiel

Daniel

Hosea

Joel

Amos

Jonah

Micah

Haggai

Zechariah

Malachi

NEW TESTAMENT

Matthew

Mark

Luke

John

Acts of the Apostles

Romans

1 Corinthians

2 Corinthians

Galatians

Ephesians

Philippians

Colossians

1 Timothy

Hebrews

James

1 Peter

1 John

2 John

Revelation

Index of Featured Scripture Passages

Matthew

Mark

Luke

John

About the Author

Meg Hunter-Kilmer is a missionary and storyteller who travels the world telling people about the fierce and tender love of God. She has two theology degrees from the University of Notre Dame and is the author of four books about Scripture and the saints, including *Saints Around the World* and *A Year in the Word Catholic Bible Journal.* Meg has given talks to widely varied audiences in nearly every state (plus over a dozen countries) and currently works as a campus minister at the University of Notre Dame. When she's not obsessively googling obscure saints, trying to convince people to read Scripture, or driving appalling distances while listening to audiobooks on double speed, she loves watching the Olympics and spending time with her nieces, nephews, and godchildren.